Susanna Rowson

Twayne's United States Authors Series

Pattie Cowell, Editor

Colorado State University

TUSAS 498

SUSANNA ROWSON
(1762-1824)
Watercolor portrait reproduced by permission
of the Susanna Haswell Rowson Collection,
Clifton Waller Barrett Library,
University of Virginia Library

Susanna Rowson

By Patricia L. Parker

Salem State College

Twayne Publishers • Boston

Susanna Rowson

Patricia L. Parker

Copyright © 1986 by G.K. Hall & Co.
All Rights Reserved
Published by Twayne Publishers
A Division of G.K. Hall & Co.
70 Lincoln Street
Boston, Massachusetts 02111

Copyediting supervised by Lewis DeSimone
Book production by Elizabeth Todesco
Book design by Barbara Anderson

Typeset in 11 pt. Garamond
by P&M Typesetting, Inc., Waterbury, Connecticut

Printed on permanent/durable acid-free paper
and bound in the United States of America

Library of Congress Cataloging in Publication Data

Parker, Patricia L.
    Susanna Rowson.

    (Twayne's United States authors series; TUSAS 498)
    Bibliography: p. 137
    Includes index.
    1. Rowson, Mrs., 1762–1824—Criticism and
interpretation. I. Title. II. Series.
PS2736.R3Z74   1986   813'.2   85-27311
ISBN 0-8057-7458-0

Contents

About the Author

Patricia L. Parker teaches English at Salem State College in Salem, Massachusetts. She received her B.A. in 1963 from Western Maryland College, her M.A. in 1964 from the University of Chicago, and her Ph.D. in 1981 from New York University. In 1982–83 she was a Fulbright professor at Kyung Hee University in Seoul, Korea, and in 1983 she lived and taught in Japan. In addition to her interest in American literature, she enjoys teaching English as a second language. Her other publications include *Charles Brockden Brown: A Reference Guide* (G.K. Hall, 1980) and *Early American Fiction: A Reference Guide* (G.K. Hall, 1984). Patricia Parker lives in Marblehead, Massachusetts, with her husband and daughter.

Preface

Susanna Haswell Rowson (1762–1824), the first American woman of letters, wrote the earliest American best-seller, *Charlotte Temple*. Since its first Philadelphia edition appeared in 1794, it has continued to capture the interest of the reading public and the scholar. Rowson's bibliographer described *Charlotte Temple* as "the most popular of all American novels" before *Uncle Tom's Cabin* and estimated that more than half a million readers, over a century and a half, enjoyed the novel.[1] But not content with being the first American to succeed in the literary marketplace, Rowson was also an actor, lyricist, poet, journalist, and educator. When she died in Boston in 1824, she was a Boston celebrity. Both her readers and students adored her, while Boston society acknowledged her as a prolific writer (ten novels, six theatrical works, six textbooks, two collections of poems, and countless songs) and a woman of good works. The American novel-reading public was to revere her name for decades to come. Yet today her accomplishments lie in obscurity, her name known only as the author of *Charlotte Temple*.

Rowson lived during a crucial period in our nation's history, as it turned from provincial colony to preindustrial nation. She herself strongly identified with the political objectives of the new republic and came to consider herself American despite her British birth, as she lived most of her life in this country. Her writings reflect an increasing concern with freedom and democratic principles, both politically and sexually. To study her song lyrics and theatrical compositions during the 1790s is to understand the popular taste of the American public who were trying to decide how to live with their newly acquired independence. Rowson's life demonstrates some of the experiences of the many musicians and actors who immigrated to this country after the revolution and who adapted their work to suit American audiences. Her life demonstrates also the way in which people who earned their livelihoods in the arts during this early Federal period crossed boundaries freely from one field to another, considering themselves artists and entertainers, not merely playwrights or actors, novelists or lyricists. And Rowson's career change from entertainer to headmistress epitomizes the popular emphasis on women's education that aroused so much controversy at the turn of the nineteenth century. For Rowson that career move seemed an extension of the didactic bent of all of her theatrical and literary experience. In an effort to explore some of these important aspects of this relatively little examined period in our social history, this study offers a look at Rowson's remarkable life as actress, lyricist, playwright, novelist, and educator.

To achieve some understanding of Susanna Rowson's life, I have examined not only her literary works, which have received the most notice, but also her theatrical life, for she wrote most of her novels while maintaining a rigorous acting schedule, and many of her writings were designed for the theater. While examining the facts of her life, which admittedly are scanty enough, I have tried to place events in the context of the world as Rowson found it, both in England and in the United States. Her world was peopled with theatrical figures, whose contributions to the arts in the early American republic deserve more study.

The primary purpose of this study, however, is to introduce the Rowson canon. Aside from *Charlotte Temple*, Rowson's novels have received only slight critical notice. During her lifetime a few of her novels were reviewed in British literary journals, but her first American review came only after her death.[2] Throughout the nineteenth century Rowson received only slight acknowledgment from literary critics. The influential Evert and George Duyckinck included her poetry in their 1855 *Cyclopedia of American Literature* and pronounced her feminism mild in tone compared with the poetry and fiction of their contemporaries.[3] The first extensive treatment of Rowson's life and works appeared in 1870 by Elias Nason, a minister and writer who shared Rowson's interests in education, music, and fiction. Nason wrote a biography as romantic as any of the subject's own novels, drawing upon letters from students and the novels themselves and evaluating her fiction on moral, not literary grounds. Many of the American literature textbooks which began to proliferate during the last quarter of the nineteenth century placed *Charlotte Temple* in the canon of American literature only because of its impressive sales, but they also derided it as popular trash. Early twentieth-century critics often disapproved of Rowson. Thomas Wentworth Higginson and Henry Wolcott Boynton in 1903 objected strenuously to the subject matter of *Charlotte Temple*.[4] William Peterfield Trent and John Erskine felt obliged to acknowledge Rowson in *Great American Writers* (1912) but insisted she was read only in "unsophisticated circles."[5]

Van Doren's *American Novel* (1912) identified Rowson's readers as "housemaids and shopgirls," attracted by the writer's use of "every device known to the romancer."[6]

Despite this mixed critical reception in the last century, *Charlotte Temple* continued to be read and the "Charlotte cult" flourished. Newspaper and magazine articles introduced theories and rehashed the "facts" behind the fiction. One historian believed he identified the house where Charlotte lived in New York, and pilgrims journeyed there.[7] Charlotte's gravestone in Trinity Church became an even greater tourist attraction. In 1905 Funk and Wagnall issued a new edition of the novel with an appreciative introduction by Francis Halsey, offering information about Charlotte Stanley and John Montresor, the real people on whom the novel was supposed to have been based.[8] A study of Charlotte Temple's popular following and of the hundreds of variously illustrated paperback versions of the novel and its dramatic imitations would constitute a study in development of American popular culture for over a hundred years.

While the reading public continued to shed tears over *Charlotte Temple*, the critical public slowly began to find merit in the novel. In 1907 Lillie Deming Loshe, while advancing the study of all American literature by publishing her *Early American Novel*, made the first analysis of Rowson's style, concluding that *Charlotte Temple* had enjoyed a wide reading public because Rowson had written sensationally but simply and directly. Fred Lewis Pattee cited Rowson as a pioneer in the use of the American Revolution as background.[9] Arthur Hobson Quinn's survey of *American Fiction* found Rowson interesting for her reflection of current standards of morality and her feminism and pronounced her works of "real significance in the history of English and American fiction."[10] In 1933 Robert Vail of the American Antiquarian Society compiled an annotated bibliography of all editions of Rowson's works and included a short biography which acknowledged her musical and theatrical careers.[11] A careful and insightful reading of Rowson by another scholar during this period was offered in 1942 by Constance Rourke. Aware of the variety of Rowson's writings, Rourke found Rowson a feminist and noted her patriotism and her educational innovations but criticized her for failing to excel at any single endeavor. Other critics found merit in Rowson, and in 1964 the College and University Press published a modern edition of *Charlotte Temple*.[12] The novel today continues to be taught in college classrooms and to be read and studied.[13]

Obviously lacking in previous studies is an examination of Rowson's complete body of work—drama, poetry, journalism, song lyrics, and textbooks, as well as novels. After one hundred and sixty years it is possible to measure Rowson's achievement against her total artistic intent and to place her where she belongs in the American tradition. It is also necessary finally to introduce her complete body of works as invitation to further study. The purpose of this book is to achieve those ends.

Patricia L. Parker

Salem State College

Chronology

1762   Susanna Haswell born Portsmouth, Hampshire, England. Christened at St. Thomas' Parish Church, Portsmouth, February 25, 1762.

1767   Arrives in Boston with her father and nurse. Family settles in Nantasket, Massachusetts.

1775   Family is removed, under guard, to Hingham, Massachusetts.

1777   Family removed to Abington, Massachusetts.

1778   Upon petition by Lt. Haswell, the family is conveyed to Halifax, and then, in a prisoner exchange, sent to London.

1786   *Victoria, A Novel.* Marries William Rowson, in London.

1788   *A Trip to Parnassus; or a Critique of Authors and Performers*, a poem, published anonymously. *The Inquisitor, or the Invisible Rambler*, a collection of tales in novel form. *Poems on Various Subjects.*

1789   *The Test of Honour*, a novel, published anonymously.

1791   *Mentoria, or the Young Ladies' Friend*, a collection of tales in novel form.
Charlotte: A Tale of Truth, a novel.

1792   *Rebecca; or, The Fille de Chambre*, a novel.

1793   Contracts to join acting company of Thomas Wignell. Arrives in Philadelphia. Company moves to and opens in Annapolis. Writes *Slaves in Algiers*, published the following year.

1794   Becomes subject of pamphlet controversy between William Cobbett and John Swanwick. Writes *The Volunteers*, a farce, published the following year. "America, Commerce and Freedom," a popular song. Writes "The Standard of Liberty," a poetical address. *Trials of the Human Heart*, a novel. *The Inquisitor*, Philadelphia edition. *Charlotte, a Tale of Truth*, Philadelphia edition. *Mentoria; or, the Young Ladies Friend*, Philadelphia edition.

1796 Signs contract with J.B. Williamson of the Federal Street Theater, Boston. Moves to Boston.

1797 *Americans in England*, a comedy, performed. Makes final stage appearance, May 17. Opens the "Young Ladies' Academy," Boston.

1798 Contributes a song for celebration of Washington's birthday. *Reuben and Rachel; or, Tales of Old Times*, a novel.

1799 Writes ode for birthday of President John Adams.

1800 "An Eulogy to the Memory of George Washington, Esq.," a poem. Moves school to Medford, Massachusetts.

1802 Holds first student exhibition at Franklin Hall, Boston. Contributes articles and columns to *Boston Weekly Magazine*.

1803 Moves school to Hull mansion, Newton, Massachusetts.

1803–1804 Serialization of *Sincerity*, a novel, in *Boston Weekly Magazine*.

1804 *Miscellaneous Poems*, a collection of poetry.

1805 *An Abridgment of Universal Geography*, a textbook.

1807 *A Spelling Dictionary*, a textbook. Moves school back to Boston. Engages sister-in-law, Mary Cordis Haswell, to assist in school management.

1811 *A Present for Young Ladies*, a collection of recitations from the academy's exhibitions. Moves school to large estate on Hollis Street, Boston.

1817 Contributes articles to *New England Galaxy*.

1818 *Youth's First Steps in Geography*, a textbook.

1820 "Ode" for the anniversray of the Boston Fatherless and Widows' Society.

1822 Retires from school duties. *Biblical dialogues Between a*

Father and His Family. Exercises in History, Chronology and Biography, a textbook.

1824 Dies in Boston, March 2, aged sixty-two.

1828 *Charlotte's Daughter; or, the Three Orphans*, published posthumously.

Chapter One
Life and Times
Childhood and Youth

Susanna Haswell was born to Susanna Musgrave Haswell and William Haswell about February 5, 1762.[1] Nothing is known of her mother, who died shortly after the birth.[2] Her father, William Haswell, had been born in 1734 in Portsmouth, England, where Haswells had lived for over a hundred years. "William Haswell" was a common name in Portsmouth, and Susanna's father had brothers, aunts, uncles, and cousins living in town when he married. Another William Haswell lived next door to him on Penny Street, both in houses more modest than their neighbors.[3] Portsmouth at that time was one of four towns together constituting a large naval station and arsenal on an island of about ten square miles. Lying on the east side of the neck of Portsea Island, Portsmouth was the garrison town. Sailors, naval officers, and dockyard workers populated the town in 1762 as they had for over two hundred years. William Haswell served in his Majesty's Royal Navy, as did his brother, Robert. Their father, Robert Haswell, had served as master attendant of the royal dockyard in Gibraltar.[4]

William Haswell married Susanna Musgrave in the parish church of St. Thomas a Becket on March 3, 1761. But within a few months Susanna Haswell grew ill, and though eleven months later she gave birth to a healthy child, she survived her infant daughter by only ten days. William buried his wife on February 15, 1762 in the parish churchyard and baptized his daughter on February 25.[5] The young widowed father quickly engaged a nurse for his baby and left her with relatives when he was sent to Massachusetts the following year.

The city of Portsmouth held sights and sounds to fascinate the small child, Susanna. She daily heard street cries of the water vendors who sold water at ha'penny a bucket and offerings of bread and oysters on the streets. Walking to market, her nurse pulled her aside to avoid being run down by single horse-chairs rented by sailors for taking their girls on runs about town. Thursday market days brought the Haswells out to buy the meat, poultry, fish, eggs, butter, and vegetables sold in abundance.

At the upper end of High Street Susanna's nurse walked her past a building of which Portsmouth residents felt justifiably proud. The Portsmouth Theatre housed their very own Portsmouth company. Here the Haswells enjoyed performances by the local company two months a year and touring companies at other times. Although the Portsmouth company was acclaimed as one of the best outside of London, the Portsmouth Theatre, later immortalized by Charles Dickens in *Nicholas Nickleby*, like many others in the mid-eighteenth century conducted business illegally, for an obsolete rule outlawed any theater not patented by the king. Calling the theater a "histrionic academy" and the plays "serious and comic lectures" did not, however, prevent the local gentry and garrison officers from enjoying drama in their own rowdy fashion.[6]

No point in Portsmouth is more than a short walk from the sea. Low tide brings in sea smells across the salt marshes and mud flats. Portsmouth men in the eighteenth century derived their livings from the sea, and Portsmouth women learned to watch the horizon for returning boats. Though she later moved to another continent, Susanna Haswell Rowson always made her home near the sea.

In the American colonies William Haswell sought a home in an area as geographically similar to Portsmouth as he could find. Hull, Massachusetts, on the head of Nantasket Peninsula, lay at the entrance to Boston Harbor. Though Haswell may have performed his revenue duties in Boston, he lived in Hull throughout his American tour of duty for the British Navy. In 1765 he married Rachel Woodward, daughter of Ebenezer Woodward, a successful merchant whose ancestors had settled in Hingham in 1636. The Haswells settled down to live modestly on William's navy salary. They rented a house, purchased one cow, and performed their chores without live-in servants.[7] Two years after he married, William Haswell returned to England to bring his daughter to Massachusetts.

Susanna Haswell, aged five, embarked from the Port of Deal in October, 1766, accompanied by her nurse and her father. This journey left such an impression that Rowson recounted it in detail twenty-five years later in a novel entitled *Rebecca; or, the Fille de Chambre:*

A fair wind presently took them out of the channel, and they flattered themselves with a prosperous voyage; but these flattering appearances were soon reversed, for the wind suddenly changed, rising almost to a hurricane, so that it was impossible to pursue their intended course or return to port, and they continued tossing about in the Atlantic till the latter end of December, and then had not half made their passage, though their provision was so exhausted that they were obliged to live on a very small allowance of bread; water and salt and meat they had, and a few pease, but of these they were extremely careful.[8]

After ten weeks at sea the crew sighted another ship, flagged it down, and pleaded for food. But the ship refused to answer, and once again the desperate passengers faced death by starvation. Ten days later another ship passed, captained by a sympathetic man whose sailors fed the hungry passengers their own dinner and equipped them with provisions for their remaining journey. Rowson described movingly in *Rebecca* the sailor who brought them meat and potatoes, and the captain who refused recompense for his kindness.

The child Susanna's first sea experience had not yet ended, however. As the brig entered Boston Harbor, it was hit by wind, sleet, and snow that froze the ropes and obscured the lighthouse at the harbor entrance. When daylight brought assistance, Susanna's father dared not let his daughter descend the icy steps of the ladder to the waiting boat, nor dared he trust carrying her himself "lest a false step or slip might destroy them both" (116). But the oncoming tide required immediate action, so an old sailor suggested tying the child around the waist and lowering her down the ship's side. Like a bundle of straw Susanna Haswell arrived for the first time in America. Small wonder that shipwrecks and dangerous sea adventures occurred in six of her later novels.

Another short and mercifully uneventful boat ride brought Susanna to Nantasket. Years later she remembered the town fondly and described it also in *Rebecca*:

On the left hand of the entrance of Boston harbor is a beautiful little peninsula, called N———; it consists of two gradually rising hills, beautifully diversified with orchards, cornfields and pasture land. In the valley is built a little village, consisting of about fifty houses. . . . The neck of land which joins this peninsula is extremely narrow, and indeed is sometimes almost overflown by the tide. On one side it forms a charmingly picturesque harbour, in which are a variety of small but delightfully fertile islands, and on the other it is washed by the ocean, to which it lays open. (118)

The Haswells occupied an old house known as the minister's house, which had been first occupied by Reverend Zechariah Whitman in

1670 and by the Reverend Samuel Veazie from 1753 to 1767.[9] Situated on a slight rise, the house faced south and provided to the west a view of Hull across Nantasket harbor.

The whole peninsula housed about one hundred and seventy people in about fifty houses in 1765, though their numbers were to decline to one hundred and twenty by the outbreak of the war. *Rebecca* recalled affectionately the New England villagers as the author knew them:

The inhabitants of New England, by their hospitality and primitive simplicity of manners, revived in the mind of our heroine the golden age, so celebrated by poets. Here were no locks or bolts required, for each one, content with his own cot, coveted not the possessions of his neighbor; here should a stranger make his appearance in their little village, though unknown by all, every one was eager to shew him the most civility, inviting him to their houses, and treating him with every delicacy the simplicity of their manner of living afforded. (120)

Though less densely populated, Hull might have reminded Susanna and her father of home. The Nantasket hills contrasted to the flatness of Portsmouth, but both towns afforded their residents the traditional livelihood of shipbuilding and fishing. Along with neighboring children, Susanna could gather blackberries, whortleberries, and strawberries, and, as she got older, clams and frogs. As soon as they grew old enough, Susanna's two half brothers, Robert, born November 24, 1768 and William, Jr., born some time later, joined her in wanderings over the Nantasket hills.[10]

Of her half brothers, Rowson wrote nothing in later years suggestive of her relationship with them, and her fiction contains very few boy children or teenagers. Of her stepmother, Rowson had little to say. In a passage in *Rebecca; or, the Fille de Chambre* which Rowson specified as autobiographical, she described Mrs. Littleton, Rebecca's stepmother, as a person with "sentiments that are narrow and illiberal" and that "kind of worldly knowledge which rendered her suspicious of the integrity of every human being" (9). The heroine and her father side with one another against Mrs. Littleton, and Mrs. Littleton competes with her stepdaughter in dress and appearance (10).

Susanna Haswell early demonstrated her quickness and her love for books. Her father's library, though small, provided Homer, Spenser, Dryden, and Shakespeare.[11] In addition to her reading she enjoyed conversations with the controversial patriot, James Otis, who lived in the home of Captain Daniel Souther in Hull much of the time from 1772 to 1774. Samuel Knapp's memoir of Susanna Rowson recorded that Otis gave the young Haswell girl his "particular notice and favour, so much so that he called her his little pupil, and allowed her frequently to share his [hours] of social relaxation." Knapp further recounted that Mrs. Rowson in her later years "was fond of recurring to this intimacy, and regarded the distinction thus bestowed on her childhood as one of the proudest of her life."[12]

This idyllic childhood was interrupted by the outbreak of the Revolutionary War. Despite her youth, Susanna Haswell felt acutely a division of loyalties in the war, and this conflict of feeling so affected her imagination that she became one of the first novelists to depict the American Revolution in fiction, using the war as background for four of her later novels.

Political tensions arose early in Hull, whose population consisted almost entirely of patriots. By August 17, 1770, the town unofficially agreed to boycott British goods.[13] But Lieutenant Haswell as yet saw no cause for alarm. A jovial man who enjoyed storytelling and jests, he had easily made friends among his neighbors, though his closest friends shared British ties.[14] But war steadily drew nearer, and he heard with increasing frequency of penalties imposed on those who refused to support actively the patriot cause. Rowson described in *Rebecca* the change that occurred in her peaceful New England village:

. . . frighted at the horrid din of arms, hospitality fled her once favorite abode, mutual confidence was no more, and fraternal love gave place to jealousy, dissension, and blind party zeal. The son raised his unhallowed arm against his parent, brothers drenched their weapons in each other's blood, and all was horror and confusion. The terrified inhabitants of N——left the village and took refuge in the more interior parts of the country. (120)

When the other residents abandoned the town, the Haswells alone remained, William Haswell torn by divided loyalties. He and his family had lived in Hull for twelve years. He had married an American woman whose relations lived in nearby towns, and they had two sons born on American soil. Through his marriage Haswell had acquired American property. He thought too highly of his king to join the cause of the patriots, but allying himself with the British would require relinquishing all his property, so he maintained his neutrality, hoping some settlement would be reached. His position thus resembled that of countless others who retained their fidelity to the crown while keeping quietly at home, neither speaking out against their rebel neighbors nor taking up arms to defend their point of view.

But neutrality in a place as strategic as the Nantasket Peninsula was impossible. At the tip of the peninsula, Hull faced the channel called "Nantasket Roads," at that time the main entrance into Boston Harbor. Through Nantasket Roads passed every vessel entering or leaving the port of Boston. When the British occupied the city, all provisions for the residents, the troops, and the hundreds of Tories who flocked to the city to escape harassment in their own towns, were received through the harbor. So the Haswells watched the brigs and schooners daily passing through Nantasket Roads.

During the first year of the war Haswell worried as he noted the maritime activity and the fighting that took place on the Harbor Islands. On May 21 Grape Island was the site of a skirmish. On May 27 Susanna and her parents watched a British schooner and several barges approach Hog Island, one of the islands lying between Nantasket and the mainland which had long been used for pasturage by Hull residents. The Haswells heard shots as the boat and barges were fired upon by colonial soldiers sent to remove livestock lest the British take it for food. Two days later, they saw the flames as the schooner burned.[15] Tension mounted, and William Haswell perhaps felt that he should have heeded warnings to emigrate to England while he could.

In June a party of American soldiers marched through Hull and took Lieutenant Haswell a temporary prisoner while they carried out their intended mission. As Rowson related the incident later, the troops crossed Nantasket beach with their whaleboats intending to destroy the lighthouse. They succeeded and crossed Nantasket on their return, victorious but fearful of being pursued. In July another fight occurred at the Boston lighthouse and this time brought a group of retreating British through the Haswell property. Major Tupper stopped at the Haswell house to leave a wounded soldier, who died within a few hours. Susanna helped her father bury the soldier in their backyard. Thus the young Susanna Haswell learned of war.[16] Although her father's standing among the people of Hull prevented any harassment by the local Committee of Safety during the first year of war, inevitably the time came when he could no longer remain immune. When he finally requested permission to return to England, the patriots refused, perhaps hoping to make a profitable prisoner exchange, for soon the entire Haswell family was taken prisoner.[17] On October 28, 1775 a small guard of American soldiers removed the Haswells—William and Rachel, Rachel's mother Elizabeth, Susanna, and the two small boys—from their home and escorted them to Hingham, a town only a few miles inland. Here they lived in a house previously owned by Stephen Lincoln, their food and firewood paid for at public expense. Sympathetic friends assisted them, but William Haswell felt demoralized and his wife grew ill. Thirteen months later (November 11, 1776) William had to petition for more assistance. On November 26, 1776 the Massachusetts House of Representatives, known as the Great and General Court, directed the selectmen of Hingham to supervise care of the Haswells,[18] but such a directive was very likely ignored. Boards of Selectmen notoriously disregarded orders from the legislature, and Hingham's selectmen had enough war-related financial worries just then. The support of this loyalist and his family seemed an unnecessary expense. Further, local authorities had found Haswell's presence increasingly troublesome for the past year. In January of 1776 Perez Morton, Deputy Secretary to the Massachusetts Council, reported that Haswell had proven unfriendly to colonial interests, "frequently making such false representations among the inhabitants as tend to cause divisions, to strengthen our enemies, to intimidate and weaken our friends." The Massachusetts Council directed Benjamin Lincoln to take the matter to General Washington, "and request that he would direct that said Haswell, with his family, be removed to some inland town, or otherways disposed of, as his Excellency shall think proper."[19] Haswell's days of neutrality had ended.

On December 5, 1777 the General Court directed the Haswells' removal to Abingdon, still further inland, and directed the Abingdon selectmen to receive the loyalist and his family, providing them with "proper support" at the expense of the Great and General Court. Susanna Rowson recounted this second move later in *Rebecca*, fictionalizing her own family in the characters of the Abthorpes, a retired army lieutenant, his ailing wife, and two girls. This time, Susanna, now fifteen, took the primary responsibility for loading their diminished belongings into the wagon. In the midst of a heavy snowstorm the journey took all day. The small house that awaited them in Abingdon had dirt floors and unprotected windows that let in the wind and snow. But their arrival was brightened by the appearances of their friends Mr. Levitt and Captain Barker, who brought food, started their fire, and attempted to tighten the drafty cottage. For such kindnesses the Haswells remembered their friends the rest of their lives.[20] The Haswells subsisted the winter of 1777-78 on Indian bread and potatoes cooked over fires Susanna built with wood she gathered from the surrounding trees. Both Rachel and William grew ill.

With the defeat of Burgoyne at Saratoga that winter, Haswell realized too late that his hopes for a settlement would never be realized and that the Americans would very likely win their independence. When he could no longer expect the support or even tolerance of the people around him, he had little choice but to leave. He petitioned the legislature in May 1778 for permission to take his family to Nova Scotia, where a prisoner exchange could be made. On May 30 the General Court granted him permission, the trip to be paid at public expense, and soon the Haswells sailed on the *Industry* for Halifax.[21] There Haswell was exchanged for Philip Duval or Deval, captain of the American privateer, the *Rattlesnake*.[22] Before the end of the summer, William, Rachel, Susanna, and the two boys landed at Hull-upon-Humber where they recovered for a while before moving on to London.

Her American experience had deeply impressed Susanna Haswell, and she would recall many of these childhood episodes in her later fiction. But more significantly, these years in the Massachusetts colony, despite the wartime misfortunes, had taught her to respect Americans. When she returned in later years as an entertainer, she confidently knew her audience.

A Youth in London

This eviction from what she had until now considered home proved another significant influence upon Susanna Haswell's career. In London the Haswells joined the hundreds of other refugees from America, perhaps those from New England who tended to gather in Westminster. Here they met others who had suffered similarly, or worse. At first the refugees waited for the war to end, that they might return to their homes and occupations. To pass the time they explored London, walking its parks, viewing the public monuments, visiting the acrobatic exhibitions at Sadler's Wells and Astley's Amphitheater, and strolling through the pleasure gardens of Vauxhall and Ranelagh. From September to May the London theater season offered to the dislocated Americans an entertainment unlike any they had known. Here

Susanna Haswell saw her first theatrical performances, probably at the spacious Drury Lane or Covent Garden theaters where Americans attended most frequently. For a shilling or two Susanna and her father could enjoy a performance that lasted from three-and-a-half to five-and-a-half hours, beginning with music that was followed by a five-act play, entr'act entertainment, and finally an afterpiece of farce or pantomime. The famous Garrick had just retired, but Sarah Siddons was approaching the height of her career. Frances Abington, Dorothea Jordan, Isabella Mattocks, Ann Pitt, and Elizabeth Pope delighted and impressed Susanna Haswell with their comic arts. And the plays of Hannah Cowley, Elizabeth Inchbald, and Harriett Lee first prompted her to consider writing for the stage herself. Her first publication, *A Trip to Parnassus* (1784), reflected the breadth of her experiences as viewer and critic and demonstrated the farsightedness with which she could evaluate talents of actors and playwrights.

The details of these years in Susanna Haswell's life remain obscure. At sixteen she became the chief financial support of her family. Her father, aged forty-four, suffering the physical and psychological effects of his detention, was no longer able to serve the Royal Navy and was to spend years attempting to receive retirement pay and recompense from the British government for his losses. Rachel Haswell was ill, and of course, Robert and William, Jr., were as yet too young to contribute much to the family coffers. A third son, John Montresor, was born sometime after the family's arrival in England and added to their financial burden. Many of Rowson's fictional characters are young women forced to seek employment to support themselves and sometimes their aging parents. All of these young women regard work as a valuable, indeed ennobling, middle-class virtue, and they enter the working world with pride and enthusiasm. With equal pride and determination they meet its disappointments.

Susanna Haswell found herself particularly well suited for teaching. In addition to her youth and enthusiasm, she could bring to such a position the accomplishments valued by middle-class society. She could conduct herself with propriety, converse intelligently and with charm, sing, perhaps play a keyboard, and sew plain and fancy needlework. She loved books and was as well read as any self-educated woman who had relied upon a father's moderately good library. More important, she was and continued to be throughout her life genuinely concerned about girls' education. In the preface to the 1814 edition of *Rebecca; or, the Fille de Chambre*, the author claimed the scene describing young Rebecca as the maligned governess was autobiographical, so we can assume young Haswell did in fact teach at some time. No real evidence exists, however, to indicate where or for whom Susanna Haswell worked after her return to England.[23]

Another field open to the young woman was public entertainment. Acting jobs paid little and were difficult to get, but songwriting offered another source of income, as Vauxhall Gardens often needed new material to supply the London public with steady musical entertainment. Susanna Haswell wrote lyrics for Vauxhall, and in a few years also began writing novels, which satisfied her desire both to teach and to entertain.[24]

With the coming of peace between the colonies and Great Britain, William Haswell and other refugees sought to recoup the financial losses they had suffered from the war. On January 28, 1786, the Massachusetts loyalists living in London gathered at the house of Sir William Pepperell on Winpole Street to discuss a possible petition to Parliament for a complete and quick restitution. In July Parliament established a five-member commission to investigate the loyalists' claims in detail. Most loyalists spent considerable time and effort collecting evidence to support their claims, locating witnesses, and copying all documents in quintuplicate. On February 10, 1786, Susanna's father appeared before the commission for a hearing, armed with papers signed by Samuel Thaxter and others confirming his imprisonment. Haswell claimed a loss of £2,037. He received £430, less £4 10s for his pension. He also received a pension of £40 from 1784 until his death, which together with his retirement allowance of £50 from the navy meant that he could support his family once again.[25] With this income, William Haswell, like many American refugees, chose to settle in England rather than return to America.

Early Career

In 1786 Susanna Haswell married William Rowson, a hardware merchant who also occasionally played trumpet, sang, and acted on stage.[26] She may have married as a result of parental pressure, or her efforts to support herself may not have succeeded as she had hoped, leading her to seek marriage for economic support. The heroine in the autobiographical novel *Sarah* (1813) describes her decision to marry without love:

I found I must accede to his proposals, or be thrown on the world, censured by my relations, robbed of my good name, and being poor, open to the pursuits and insults of the profligate. One thing which encouraged me to hope I might be tolerably happy in this union was—though my heart felt no strong emotions in his favor, it was totally free from all partiality towards any other. He always appeared good-humored and obliging; and though his mind was not cultivated, I thought time might improve him in that particular.[27]

Time did not improve him, however, and the marriage proved far from ideal. As a forceful and active woman, Susanna Rowson dominated the relationship. Her earnings supported both of them, and her career determined how and where they lived. At best William served as helpmeet, occasional assistant, the husband required of any proper lady. At worst he brought her unhappiness and impeded her career. In later years he had trouble holding a job, and he drank heavily. Susanna Rowson remained married to William, however, and they always lived under the same roof. But she bore him no children, though she did raise his illegitimate son, and in her last years the marriage gave her a sense of failure which led to loneliness and depression. The title page of *Sarah* contains this line from John Gregory's *Legacy*: "Do not marry a fool; he is continually doing absurd and disagreeable things, for no other reason but to shew he dares do them."[28]

Whatever marital unhappiness lay ahead of her, Rowson found at the start of the marriage the excitement of a new life, for with William she began her career as a public performer. William had some connection with Covent Garden from 1782 through 1793, though he was not a stage performer. His sister Elizabeth appeared there occasionally as dancer and minor actress. Susanna Rowson's first stage appearances are unknown, but evidence does exist that she performed with a company of London actors at Brighton in the summer of 1786. Quite likely both Rowsons performed with provincial companies when they could not find opportunities in London. There, all aspiring young actors wanted to try their luck, but since neither Susanna nor William had great talent, the young couple perhaps joined a group of "strolling players," acting companies which called themselves by the names of the towns where they had headquarters. The Rowsons could have joined a company from Bath, Norwich, York, Liverpool, Manchester, Bristol, or Newcastle, all of which operated under royal patent. With a town company, the couple would have traveled to surrounding towns for varying periods of time ranging from two to four months.

As a neophyte, Susanna Rowson had to work for a six-month probationary period without salary.[29] After this period of unpaid apprenticeship, the Rowsons could earn about thirteen shillings sixpence a week each playing in towns outside London. That wage compared favorably with a laborer who might earn an average of eight or nine shillings a week, though it seemed slight in contrast to the hundreds of pounds earned by the favorites of the London stage.

Both William and Susanna realized early that they would never become exceptional performers, though perhaps because of her diligence, Susanna was the better of the two, as evidenced by her more frequent performances and her more significant roles. William's love of music proved an asset in ballad operas and plays with musical accompaniment as well as in entr'act entertainment, for music was growing increasingly popular in theater. Susanna supplemented her rather average ability for acting, singing, and pantomime with a conscientious effort at learning her parts and attending rehearsals, behavior which distinguished her from many of her colleagues. Actors in both London and provincial companies frequently had neither ability nor inclination to work. They often arrived late at rehearsal or rehearsed not at all, with predictably disastrous consequences at performance time. Companies often performed a different play each night or every two nights, so every member of the company might be responsible for over twenty parts at a time.[30] Susanna quickly learned the virtues of hard work between performances, and she admired others who studied their parts with care. During performance she would not condescend to behave as many did, laughing and swearing at the audience, or ad-libbing to draw attention to herself. Though she shared other actors' annoyance when the audience talked—or shouted or threw objects onto the stage—she considered acting a respectable profession and could only wish that all her colleagues regarded it as she did.

Two years after her first known stage performance Susanna Rowson felt sufficiently well acquainted with London theater to write a short book about it. At twenty-six she displayed the confidence that would characterize all her future endeavors. Though her own experiences cannot have been extensive, and she had not performed in London, she evaluated with assurance and accuracy the writers and actors associated with Covent Garden in *A Trip to Parnassus* (1788), the first of a lifetime of publications.

To what extent was young Rowson jeopardizing her reputation with this public association with the theater? The English theatrical world of the 1780s was becoming a middle-class amusement. Daily attendance had doubled from 1742 to 1775, requiring enlargements of the patent houses. By 1781 Drury Lane could seat about two thousand, and Covent Garden was remodeled in 1784 to accommodate three thousand.[31] As audiences grew, so did the general reputation of people associated with theater. David Garrick and even lesser names moved in the best social, literary, and artistic circles of their times. Women too were accepted, and although some found their affairs and illegitimate children as highly publicized as their stage roles, most led conventionally virtuous married lives. Married couples often acted in the same company, and even actor families, such as the Kembles, became known. It would not have appeared unusual or unseemly for an officers' daughter, married to a man who held some association with the theater, to identify herself with a theater company and even to appear herself on stage. Every stage appearance, however, subjected her to potential insult and injury from outspoken audiences and to the malicious tongue-wagging of those who regarded actresses as women of ill repute.

Susanna Rowson finally appeared in her only known London performance on October 15, 1792, when a company took over the Haymarket to give a benefit. In the afterpiece *Who's the Dupe*, Susanna Rowson played Charlotte.

Throughout this period of attempts at acting Rowson busily plied her pen. In 1786 she published her first novel, *Victoria, A Novel*, followed two years later by *The Inquisitor*, a loosely structured, picaresque series of short stories or scenes related by a narrator. Both novels received only cursory reviews. In 1789 Rowson published *Mary; or, the Test of Honour* anonymously, posing in the preface as a new author. The two reviews of this work might have persuaded a less-determined author to cease, but Rowson persisted. In 1791 she published *Mentoria*, a collection of ten letters, three short stories, and one essay, compiled, the author confides in a footnote, for women who do not read novels. And in the same year she published the book that was ultimately to bring her fame, *Charlotte: A Tale of Truth*. But even a favorable review did not bring income, for publishers paid women authors only small sums for the manuscript, regardless of the number of copies the book ultimately sold.

In 1793 William, Susanna, and William's younger sister, Charlotte, traveled to Edinburgh in hopes of stage success. There the three of them joined the company of Harriet Bennett Pye Esten, an actor and newly assumed manager of the Theatre Royal in Shakespeare Square. However, neither William nor Charlotte actually performed. Susanna played twice in January and then sat idle for six weeks. Between March 18 and May 4 she performed in six plays. But the company was beset by competition and financial problems, and the Rowsons received little pay. By the end of the season Susanna Rowson could foresee no future for herself and her husband on the English stage. Their best efforts had failed, and they could not earn a living. When company manager Thomas Wignell appeared with an offer to sign the three of them on with his American company, Susanna, William, and Charlotte accepted with alacrity.

American Theatrical Career

Thomas Wignell had traveled to London in 1792 to scout for actors for his new Philadelphia Theater. A talented actor himself, Wignell had in 1791 resigned from Hallam's Old American Company and had entered into partnership with the musician Alexander Reinagle to establish a new theater. This new house would compete with the Old American Company at the Southwark Theater, which had first opened in 1766, then closed along with all other colonial theaters during the Revolution, and recently opened again to a growing audience. The closing of all theaters during the Revolution had sent many actors, including Wignell himself, out of the country to find work, and too few returned to meet the growing demand for entertainment in the cities of the eastern seaboard. Thus Wignell had traveled to England to create a new company of English recruits.

Wignell proved an effective scout. Onto the ship the *George Barcley* he brought men and women who were to become the mainstays of the American theater for the next few decades, among them several married couples such as the Rowsons. Miss Broadhurst, a singer, Mr. and Mrs. Broadhurst, Mr. and Mrs. Marshall, Mr. and Mrs. Warrell, and about fifty others made up the immigrant company that arrived in Philadelphia in the fall of 1793.[32]

The well-planned opening of the New Theater, however, was postponed by an outbreak of yellow fever. The entire city had shut down and most of the population had fled. The company was shuttled off to New Jersey and finally made its debut in Annapolis, where Rowson appeared in the farce, *Who's the Dupe?* by Hannah Cowley. Not until January, 1794, did the company finally move to Philadelphia, where an as-yet-incomplete but nonetheless large and imposing theater building awaited them. To enthusiastic and demonstrative audiences in their first four-and-a-half month season Rowson performed thirty-five roles. In the second season she worked an only slightly less grueling schedule, learning twenty-two additional parts.

With her usual vigor, Rowson pursued other activities besides acting. To the music of Alexander Reinagle, she wrote lyrics. One of her first songs, written a month after the theater's opening, was "America, Commerce, and Freedom," a ballet pantomime produced by the company choreographer, William Francis. The lyrics demonstrate Rowson's sense of rhythm and her quickly acquired sense of American patriotism together in a catchy, sailor's drinking song. Thus from the start Rowson collaborated with Reinagle and other immigrant musicians whose work constituted a significant part of American theater music during this early period of the republic.

In the same year Rowson wrote her first American plays, *Slaves in Algiers* and *The Volunteers*. She also published American editions of *Charlotte, A Tale of Truth*; *Rebecca; or, The Fille de Chambre*; *Mentoria*; and *The Inquisitor*. The following year she wrote *The Female Patriot*, an adaptation of a play by Philip Massinger, and "The Standard of Liberty," a poetical address presented to the U.S. Army. Unfortunately, the fiction she produced that year evidenced her preoccupation with other affairs, and *Trials of the Human Heart* appeared as a hastily written, flawed novel. But if she was too busy to produce careful fiction, she knew how to turn out good songs, and the Philadelphia New Theater audience frequently heard new numbers from "Mrs. Rowson." Many of her songs were published separately and sold as sheet music.

Rowson's two years with the Philadelphia theater thus proved productive ones. For the Wignell-Reinagle company she produced at least three plays, several songs, and one poetical address while performing in over thirty-five roles. Though as a playwright she had only moderate ability, as a lyricist she had real talent. Her affinity for music had induced her to begin writing songs very early in her career, and she would continue for as long as she lived. Because her dramatic talents were limited, she had found herself participating in musical pieces more often than in serious drama. She also found herself surrounded by musicians, even after she moved to Philadelphia. Many composers whose music was being sung and played in American theaters in the last decade of the eighteenth century were immigrants like Rowson whose chief livelihood derived from the theater. Musicians such as Peter van Hagen, James Hewitt, Raynor Taylor, Victor Pelissier, and Benjamin Carr gave lessons, held concerts, opened music stores and musical publishing houses while writing music for the theaters. Like actors, these musicians moved freely from city to city, and their circle of musical colleagues grew large. With them Rowson felt at home, for with many she shared not only a common immigrant experience but also a theatrical background. These musicians constituted her colleagues and friends, both in Philadelphia and then in Boston for many years.

Thus, though her stay in Philadelphia had been brief, Rowson had established herself there as a professional actress. Though not a "star" performer, she had gained experience and popularity as a supporting actress, and she had acquired a popular following through her writings for the stage. She had also gained confidence in her ability to judge the playgoing public. She had become, as some editions of her books would identify her for years to come, "Mrs Rowson, of the New Theater, Philadelphia."

Despite Rowson's high level of productivity during her stay in Philadelphia, she had not been entirely happy. Her husband proved so inept on stage that Wignell took him off the acting list and relegated him to prompter. But William did not hold even that position for long and was soon replaced by someone with more experience. In September, 1796, the Rowsons joined seven other actors in a defection from the Philadelphia company to the Boston company.[33] Although they had always received their salaries, Rowson and her colleagues sensed financial trouble, brought on by yellow fever outbreaks, competition from the other Philadelphia theater, and expenses incurred by the production of operas rather than ordinary plays, and they had little to gain by remaining with a company going bankrupt.

Susanna Rowson had at least one good personal reason for feeling drawn to Boston—the presence of her two half brothers. Robert Haswell, now twenty-eight, had written in January 1796, the first time she had heard from him in eight years. Though he planned to set off on another sea voyage by spring, he hoped to return to Boston in a few years to buy a farm. His sailing years had severely impaired his health, and he wrote wistfully of settling down. Their younger brother Bill, also a seaman, was attending school in Boston, studying navigation. Susanna wrote back to Robert asking him about Boston as a place to live and asking his advice about a theater company there. Robert sent his reply via John Williamson, the manager of the Boston Federal Street Theater, but warned his sister that Boston was expensive. And though he also warned of the impending construction of a competing second theater, he nonetheless urged her to move, "for it would be in my honour to add something to your happiness." To encourage her, he alluded to the reputation her books had already established for her.[34] When Williamson's season opened in September, the Rowsons numbered among the company.

In Boston Rowson again found herself in a large and elegantly appointed theater house. She felt pleased with her surroundings and even more pleased when she learned the policies of the theater's trustees, who, having overcome Boston's fear of immorality, now insisted on approving all of the manager's appointments and dismissing promptly any actor found guilty of unsuitable conduct (which meant that William Rowson would have to behave himself). In a further effort to placate a wary public, the trustees had established the position of marshall for the purpose of keeping order both in and out of the building. This dignified bouncer received a weekly salary higher than anyone on the stage or in the orchestra.

Rowson recognized familiar faces among the Boston company, which like most American companies was filled with English immigrants. From her fellow actors Rowson learned of the theater's standing in the city. She was told that the theater enjoyed an uneasy truce with the forces of religion in Boston. A few blocks up the street stood the Federal Street Church, led by the outspoken Reverend Jeremy Belknap, and the trustees had agreed never to allow theater performances on the same evening his church held services. She was more surprised to learn that attendance at the theater was a political statement. The previous manager, "Colonel" Tyler, had made public his Federalist sympathies through his selection of plays, and the new manager, John Williamson, had done nothing to change the public image. Thus anyone seen going in the doors of the theater was known as a Federalist.[35]

Despite political, religious, and moral restrictions, all three Rowsons found satisfaction in the roles they were given under Williamson's direction. Both William and Charlotte played more important roles than they had previously, and Susanna added a number of characters to her repertoire. As usual, however, one occupation did not fully satisfy this ambitious woman, so she also began writing songs. Shortly after her arrival she had met musicians who constituted part of Boston musical circles, many of whom were English and European immigrants: Samuel Arnold, Oliver Holden, James Hewitt, Peter Van Hagen, and Gottlieb Graupner. Rowson was soon writing lyrics for the songs of these composers, and she also produced one dramatic piece called *Americans in England*. In addition she wrote one novel during her stay with the Federal Street Theater, a work that anticipated her next career as teacher and headmistress. *Reuben and Rachel; or, Tales of Old Times* appeared in 1798, published by Manning & Loring of Boston.

But as the season progressed, Rowson saw her brother's warning about the impending difficulties of the theater confirmed. Evening after evening they played to a half-empty house. On December 26 their problems were compounded by the opening of a second Boston theater, the Haymarket, near the corner of Tremont and Boylston Streets. Though the Federal Street Theater trustees fought back by offering free tickets to anyone promising never to set foot in the competing theater, both companies suffered. By the end of the season neither one could pay its bills. By July John Williamson departed for North Carolina, an the company members scattered to seek employment where they could.[36]

Career in Education

At the age of thirty-five Susanna Haswell Rowson decided to end her theatrical career. Never happy with the social position of actors, she sought both money and respectability, neither of which she could find in the theater. In November, 1797, Susanna Rowson opened her own school, "Mrs. Rowson's Young Ladies' Academy," on Federal Street, near the theater. She chose Boston as the city in which to settle and begin her new career for several reasons. It was, in a sense, her American home, not far from Nantasket where she had grown up. It was the city where her brothers planned to live, if and when they ever ceased their wanderings. It was, moreover, the American city that most resembled an English town, its precarious and winding streets and alleys named Frog Lane, Distillery-House Square, White-Bread Alley, and Oliver's Dock, its unnumbered houses and unpaved roads recalling England for Rowson as Philadelphia had not.

Boston held the additional appeal of a center for learning, having established by this time not only colleges but also various general educational, cultural, and historical institutions: the American Academy of Arts & Sciences (1780); the Massachusetts Medical Society (1787); the Boston Library Society (1792) the Massachusetts Agricultural Society (1796); the Massachusetts Historical Society (1791). In advance of the lyceum movement, individuals and institutions frequently held public lectures on a variety of subjects. Rowson also liked the fact that here the clergy still held moral sway, and the people responded favorably to her books with their moral messages. Though the city did not offer all the cultural opportunities of Philadelphia, it did have a museum, the two theaters, and especially important for William Rowson, an active group of musicians who performed in Pond Street. One of these musicians was Gottlieb Graupner, who had performed during Rowson's season with the Federal Street Theater and who planned now to remain in the city, give lessons, and establish an orchestra. Gottlieb Graupner and his wife, Catherine Hillyer, also a singer and theatrical performer, became Rowson's closest friends.

Rowson's decision to open her own school fulfilled her lifelong interest in women's education. This field would increasingly in the next few decades come to be regarded as "one of the most delicate and responsible, . . . to which a female can aspire."[37] Rowson was eminently well suited for the position of headmistress. Though not tall, she carried herself with dignity and, with her full figure, looked imposing. Her "elegant manners, lively imagination, fine conversational powers, and affectionate disposition" appealed to both students and parents, so that gradually she attracted to her school the best families in Boston and environs. Her theatrical experience had taught her to entertain as well as instruct, and she knew the appeal of music. In 1799 she introduced a pianoforte into her school, an event that created excitement and added to her prestige. She called upon her theatrical colleague, R. Laumont, to teach music, and she herself sometimes joined her students in their dancing lessons. Admiring students found her "a light and pretty dancer."[38]

While administering an efficient and educationally sound school, Rowson made a conscious attempt to win a place in Boston society.

Sensitive to the city's intense political and patriotic interests, she wrote and circulated a song for the celebration of Washington's birthday in 1798 and an ode on the birthday of John Adams. She also wrote a "Eulogy to the Memory of George Washington, Esq." Always interested in the sea, she also wrote patriotic songs inspired by the encounter between the frigate *Constellation* and the French warship *Insurgent* on February 9, 1799.

In 1800 Susanna Rowson moved her academy from Boston to Medford, a suburb about five miles northwest of the city. The move placed the school in the country, for Medford could boast only about 120 houses with almost as many barns, and only three shops. In this lovely town stretched along the Mystic River Rowson leased from Joseph Wyman a large and stately home with two large gardens in front fringed by two long avenues of trees leading from High Street to the greenhouse in the rear.[39] Medford offered opportunities for Rowson because it boasted prosperous residents. To Rowson's academy came the daughters of the Brooks, the Bishops, the Tufts, the Blanchards, and the Halls, all of whom considered themselves the finest families in New England. To reassure their parents, she denied her own preference for the Episcopal Church and took her young ladies to the Congregational First Church of Medford. She also added to her curriculum painting and drawing, embroidery "and its various branches," and French, and charged extra for each subject. This one-time actor who had charmed audiences from the stage now spent hours in parlor conversation with the Congregational minister and Dr. John Brooks, a successful physician and influential Federalist who later became govenor of Massachusetts. Even William made attempts to live up to his wife's reputation by becoming in 1802 a naturalized citizen in order to take a clerkship in the Customs Service. He kept this job for as long as his wife lived, but his irresponsible behavior displeased his employers.[40]

In 1803 Rowson moved to Newton and opened a school there. Her move may have initiated in an offer of a house from William Hull, a well-to-do Revolutionary War hero then practicing law in a large house he had built in 1799. Newton was less rural than Medford but still several miles from the center of Boston. Its village square was surrounded by small shops and markets and a single tavern. Near the square stood Murdock's store, where residents could buy groceries and where farmhands stopped twice a day, English fashion, for their dram of rum.[41] In Newton Rowson shared responsibilities as headmistress with her sister-in-law, Mary Cordis Haswell, from Reading. Mary Cordis had married Robert Haswell on October 10, 1798, and six months later Robert had sailed out on the U.S. frigate *Boston*, as first lieutenant. His wife had taken comfort in Rowson's company, especially on her first anniversary while Robert was engaged in the battle between the *Boston* and a French national corvette. On April 13, 1801 Robert had left the navy to command the *Louisa*, a Boston boat bound for the Northwest coast, China, and return. Robert hoped to earn a sizable sum of money on this voyage and then settle down with Mary and their two daughters. But his plans went down with him, for his ship was last heard from in August, 1801.[42] Mary and her two baby girls, Mary and Rebecca, moved in with Susanna and William, and Mary Haswell helped Rowson manage the school.[43] The Newton academy students included three daughters of William Hull, three young ladies from the West Indies, and the daughters of Governor Claiborne of South Carolina.

Perhaps because of the free time Mary's assistance allowed her, Rowson was able to return to writing for the first time since she had opened her school, and in 1805 she published *An Abridgment of Universal Geography*, a textbook. Her maritime family had instilled in her an interest in the globe, in foreign lands, and in the arts of navigation, and she always considered geography a primary part of her curriculum for young women. She also included in the text commentary on the position of women in various eastern countries.

In 1807 Rowson moved her academy again, this time back into Boston. The city offered advantages for both the school and for the Rowsons personally. There she could hire music and dancing teachers from the theater; she engaged Gottlieb Graupner to teach music, and she enlisted as dancing master the second violinist from the theater orchestra. There she could more easily escort her students to theatrical and musical events, and she herself could attend regularly the many musical entertainments in which her friends performed. For the first four years she leased a mansion on Washington Street near Roxbury Gate. The house contained three parlors, nine bedrooms, a school hall, a dining room, two kitchens, a washhouse, a barn, stables, and a garden.[44] From this house Rowson produced *The Spelling Dictionary* (1807).

With this return to the city, William Rowson began to take an active role in musical affairs. He played the trumpet for the Boston Philharmonic Society organized in 1810 or 1811 by Gottlieb

Graupner; he became a founding member of the Handel and Haydn Society in 1815, and he also played with a group known as the Park Street Choir.[45]

An indication of Rowson's financial success is her purchase in 1809 of a house and lot on Hollis Street in Boston for the sum of $4,600, a considerable amount for property at the time.[46] At about this time she also adopted and supported Fanny Mills, daughter of an actor who had died, and Susan Johnston, daughter of her sister-in-law, Charlotte. William's illegitimate son had by this time left home, perhaps to go to sea; he was at any rate no longer a member of the household.[47] The Rowson school did not actually move into Hollis Street until 1811, suggesting that the house needed remodeling or perhaps replacement with a new building. The school remained in the Hollis Street house for the rest of Rowson's life. (Mary Haswell continued in the Washington Street school and managed it on her own.) At this final residence Rowson continued the activities for which she had acquired her local reputation. Here she wrote her textbooks, *A Present for Young Ladies* (1811), *Exercises in History, Chronology, and Biography* (1822), and *Biblical Dialogues* (1822); and her last novels, *Sarah; or, the Exemplary Wife*, and *Charlotte's Daughter; or, The Three Orphans*. She wrote poems and essays for *The New England Galaxy* and she wrote poems for public occasions. She continued to follow American politics with concern, and when peace was declared in 1805, she decorated her house with pictures and banners.[48] Although her adopted daughter, Fanny Mills, did not become the close and affectionate relation she had hoped, she continued to take great pleasure in close relationships with her students.

Last Years

In 1822 ill health forced Susanna Rowson to resign from school responsibilities. Reluctantly she turned the school over to her adoptive daughter, Fanny Mills, and to her niece, Susan Johnston, daughter of Charlotte Rowson. These two women opened the spring session on April 15, with Susanna Rowson assisting only in the teaching of composition. A friend, Samuel Lorenzo Knapp, who visited her in her retirement, reported that she spent her time writing, "participating in the social intercourse of a select circle of friends, and enjoying the consolations, which arise from the review of life spent in active virtue and diffusive benevolence."[49] Aware that illness had long plagued her, he admired her ability to disguise her suffering in the presence of others.

Rowson's last years were not happy. Her father had died in 1805, and all three of her half brothers had also predeceased her. In 1821 her close friend Catherine Graupner died. Her own ill health and her unfortunate marriage weighed upon her. For years she had heard students whisper about her husband and knew that she lost respect in their eyes because she was married to him. She had remained a loyal wife and had supported him for years, even while his drinking, lack of initiative, and irresponsibility had humiliated her before her colleagues and pupils.[50] When he had fathered an illegitimate child, Rowson had taken the boy, even loving him as her own, but in her last years she no longer had the comfort of young William's love, for he had drowned in Boston Harbor sometime after 1811.[51] In the last years her husband had caused her even greater worry, for he had incurred large debts and had taken a $2500 mortgage on their Hollis Street house.[52] Recurring illnesses prevented her from earning enough to pay off the debt so that it weighed heavily on her during her last years.[53]

Susanna Rowson died March 2, 1824 and was interred in the Gottlieb Graupner family vault in St. Matthew's Church, South Boston. When the church was demolished in 1866, her remains were transferred to Mt. Hope Cemetery in Dorchester, Massachusetts, and a granite monument was erected later in Forest Hill Cemetery, Roxbury, by her descendants, Mary and Haswell C. Clarke and Ellen Murdock Osgood. Obituaries appeared in the *Boston Evening Gazette* on March 6, 1824, and in the *Columbian Centinel* March 10, 1824.

William Rowson remarried five months later and in four more years took another $2500 mortgage on the Hollis Street house and land. When he died at age seventy-seven on July 21, 1843, he left all his property to his "beloved wife," Hannah Smith Rowson.[54] The William S. Rowson who married a Pennsylvania woman in 1858 was probably the offspring of this second marriage.[55]

Susanna Rowson's works stand as a tribute to her versatility, adaptability, and remarkable productivity. Her biography stands as testimony to an industrious and generous woman who strove all her life to teach other women how to live. Her works reflect contemporary standards of literary taste and morality, but they also reflect distinctive qualities. In fiction, Rowson produced a number of heroines who overcame trials and adventures by virtue of their intelligence and practicality, models for the author's young women readers. In her textbooks she forthrightly asserted women's rights to education and depicted countless historical models of women's achievements. In her own life she demonstrated the unflagging energy and perseverance necessary for achieving fame, affluence, and influence. Susanna Rowson lived at a significant moment in American history, participating extensively in the arts of the new republic. She was one of the first women lyricists and dramatists, one of the first to write about the American Revolution in fiction, and certainly one of the first to demonstrate the self-determination and professional ambition that mark women of the late twentieth century.

Chapter Two
English Fiction

When or how Susanna Haswell began writing poetry and fiction is not known. At approximately the time she began writing the great novelists of the period had died; Fielding in 1754, Richardson in 1761, Sterne in 1768, and Smollett in 1771. The only living novelist of any stature was Fanny Burney, whose *Evelina* had been well received in 1778. Women authors were no longer regarded as monstrosities as they had been a century earlier; a number of women had published during the last decade, though their propriety in doing so had caused some controversy. Following the tradition begun by Aphra Behn (1640–1689) came Mrs. Radcliffe (1764–1823), Elizabeth Inchbald (1753–1821), Maria Edgeworth (1767–1849), and Hannah Moore (1745–1833), to name the best known. These women faced the "utter discredit of being known as a female writer of novels and romances" which induced Fanny Burney to bury her first manuscripts.[1] Nevertheless, some of them went on to write prodigious amounts of fiction: Maria Edgeworth, for example, wrote over sixty books.

These women wrote for female readers who constituted three-quarters of the novel-reading public. Though they often wrote primarily to earn money, booksellers tried to avoid paying their fees. Some booksellers offered authors as little as half a guinea per volume, with the usual price running between five and ten guineas. But prices sometimes went to £30, and Fanny Burney received £250 from Payne and Cadell in 1782 for *Cecelia*. Such possibilities lured more women into the field, especially with so few other respectable occupations available to them.[2]

Equally attractive to women were the themes and subject matter of novels as introduced by Samuel Richardson. Richardson had brought to the novel the world of the middle class and its attendant values and virtues. Who could argue that women's time was better spent in making a pudding than in scribbling, when that scribbling became a poem or story about ladies' domestic concerns? English women's novels between 1770 and 1800 dealt with the world of the home; their farthest limits extended to the opera, the debtors' prison, or the French convent finishing school. Few scenes included men (a characteristic also of Jane Austen), and male characters existed chiefly in their domestic aspects, as fathers, sons, or lovers.[3] Domestic themes lent themselves to a moral didacticism to which women readily responded. Women authors wrote to instruct their compatriots how to become "exemplary" mothers and daughters and wives.

Victoria

Susanna Haswell entered this woman's literary world, eager to earn money and a name for herself by entertaining instructively. She tried to imitate her peers by focusing primarily upon domestic matters and by advocating a prudential type of morality. She soon differed, however, from her contemporaries by creating heroines with more assertiveness and a greater sense of adventure than the passive females created by her peers. In this respect she resembled Fanny Burney whose heroines respected social norms but also believed in self-reliance. Haswell's first novel, published in 1786 shortly before she married, fit the conventional pattern of her contemporaries. The title made clear her didactic intention: *Victoria, a Novel. In Two Volumes. The Characters Taken from Real Life, and Calculated to Improve the MORALS OF THE FEMALE SEX, By Impressing Them with a Just Sense of THE MERITS OF FILIAL PIETY.*

For this first novel Haswell sought a patron who could guarantee her subscribers. By 1786 publication by subscription had gone out of fashion, and most writers no longer bothered with patronage since the growing reading public provided sufficient sales. But for her first effort Haswell preferred assistance, so she found a patron and dedicated her book to "her grace the Duchess of Devonshire."[4] Both in the dedication and in the novel Haswell praised the benevolence and virtue of the duchess. Georgiana Cavendish, wife of the fifth Duke of Devonshire, was an intelligent and educated patron of the arts and herself a writer of poems and novels. Haswell felt proud to receive the patronage of this reigning social queen who kept company with Horace Walpole, Madam D'Arblay, Charles Fox, and Richard Sheridan. The duchess helped Haswell find an impressive list of 270 subscribers, led by the names of Samuel Adams and General Burgoyne, an unlikely combination of names, perhaps, but the author held no hard feelings toward either side after the war. Haswell also obtained a number of subscribers on her own, most of them drawn from the Covent Garden Theatre. George Colman, the theater manager, and several actors and actresses including Sarah Siddons subscribed to *Victoria*. In addition, the names of "Wm. R———" and "Miss Rowson," probably William's sister, a London actress and dancer, appeared on the list. Haswell married William Rowson later that same year.

Following the convention of the time, she published *Victoria* in two volumes. She chose as her publisher J.P. Cooke, apparently not the John Cooke who operated a large and profitable bookselling and printing business on Paternoster Row, for this J.P. Cooke located at 38 Tavistock Street. Haswell found him unpleasant and would not have dealt with him had she felt more sure of herself. She described him unsympathetically in her next novel, which she took to another publisher.

The main plot of *Victoria* relates the adventures of the unfortunate young Victoria Baldwin, daughter of a deceased naval officer. Victoria at first resists an attempted seduction by the rich and handsome young Harry Finchly, only to be taken in by a sham marriage. She is soon pregnant and abandoned, and the birth of her son brings on insanity and finally death. The plot thus follows the standard tale of seduction. To this main plot are added at least five subplots and several brief stories within stories, yet all details are related clearly and the book never grows confusing. Most of the subplots reinforce the theme of filial piety, which, according to the subtitle and the epigraph from Milton, is the primary lesson the author sought to convey.

The first subplot relates the story of Lady Maskwell, who at age fourteen leaves Scotland, her mother, and nine starving brothers and sisters to seek her fortune in London. In exchange for support, she becomes the mistress of the Earl of Maskwell, who educates and eventually marries her. But Lady Maskwell becomes the female villain of the novel, consumed by greed, ambition, and deceit until she is herself finally cheated out of everything by her own accomplice. Another subplot relates the story of Bell Hartley, who caps off her winter social season in London by marrying a wealthy lord and traveling to Europe. Yet another subplot relates the story of Mary Philmore, an honest and virtuous girl who is cheated out of marriage by her own cousin Lucy. Mary's virtuous nature leads her to forgive her cousin, overcome the vicious gossip circulating about her, and finally retires to a French convent.

Several passages in *Victoria* called upon the author's own experience. Young women characters are daughters of army or naval officers, for instance, and some of them face the necessity, as Haswell had recently done, of earning a living without assistance from anyone who can provide them with a "character." The novel also includes one description of a storm at sea and several allusions to the theater. The descriptions of hotels, service, and tourist sights in Brussels and France suggest firsthand acquaintance with Continental travel, which Haswell had possibly enjoyed during her employment as governess. Allusions to the "late war with America" suggest the author's sensitivity to the ways in which the revolution had affected the lives of many British citizens. In addition, *Victoria* reflects her enthusiasm for reading, with an epigraph from Milton and quotations from or allusions to Shakespeare, Goldsmith, Prior, and Milton.

Victoria reflects a youthful experimentation in prose and poetry. Written in epistolary form like many sentimental novels of the 1870s, *Victoria* includes letters from many characters and thus various points of view. Sometimes the same event is related from two or three points of view. Letter writers' styles also vary; Victoria writes in the sentimental style, Bell Hartley writes with sarcastic humor, and Fanny Todd writes moralistic essays. The letters contain many poems, at least one of which, "To Anne," appeared later in *Mentoria*. The poems include an ode on a sunrise, a satire on a hairdresser and makeup specialist, an animal fable, and various verses in couplets. Many of the poems are in fact rhythmic songs that the letter writer tells the reader someone has set to music, though the music is not included in the novel. Haswell thus, even in this early fiction, demonstrated her love of music.

For her central theme in *Victoria* Haswell chose the didactic theme that she found in most novels of the day, filial piety. This middleclass virtue required unquestioning obedience of both sexes, though the dangers inherent in disobedience appear greater for girls than for boys. Filial obedience in the eighteenth century was part of the larger cult of submission, idealized in women's novels as a sign of spiritual grace. This virtue expressed itself not only in submission of son or daughter to parent, but of wife to husband (though never the reverse), servant to master, even friend to friend.[5] Susanna Haswell's insistence upon filial piety reflects this literary phenomenon. Although she always advocated obedience to parents, she never approved of unreasonable submission of wife to husband and eventually rejected the idea of any submission in marriage.

In *Victoria* the main plot teaches that even slight disobedience to parental instruction carries dire consequences. The title character refuses to break her mother's heart by becoming Finchly's mistress, and she lectures her lover at length on the consequences of illicit love. But she does disobey her mother by meeting Finchly secretly for several months, and, seduced by his artful persuasion, Victoria eventually runs away with her lover. Though she believes herself lawfully married, she suffers the fate of almost all seduced heroines—childbirth and death. Several subplots reinforce the same theme. Fanny Todd, younger sister of the wicked Lady Maskwell, contrasts sharply with the female villain by staying with her mother and providing the respect and care expected of a dutiful daughter. Fanny is rewarded with marriage to a good husband, who is attracted by the strength of her devotion to her mother. Two briefly narrated stories contrast the rewards of submission with the consequences of disobedience. Sukey loses her inheritance when she marries a man against her father's wishes, and she loses even her husband's love as soon as she is disinherited. Her foil, Charlotte R., rejects a young and attractive suitor to marry a man she does not love because her parents wish it. She becomes a dispenser of goods to the poor, "what the Duchess of D—— is," and leads a happy, benevolent life. Thus Haswell drives her point home through various narratives, all of them, she hopes, more persuasive than a moral lecture.

Tied to the theme of filial piety is of course the seduction theme, common to many novels of the eighteenth century. In the tradition of the Richardsonian seduction novel Victoria demonstrates that loss of virginity without the sanction of marriage, no matter how well intentioned the heroine and how extenuating the circumstances, must result in childbirth and death to the woman involved. (Charlotte Temple is the only one of Rowson's other heroines who succumbs to a seducer, and she suffers the same fate.) Victoria's only crimes are that she meets Finchly secretly against her mother's advice and that she is foolish enough to believe that anyone in clerical attire is legally qualified to perform a marriage ceremony. Rowson's later novels develop heroines too intelligent to fall for such a ruse.

Though victimized by a seducer and mother to an illegitimate child, Victoria nonetheless has the constant support of her loving mother and sister. As her later novels were to repeat, the author believed firmly in parental forgiveness. When Mrs. Baldwin learns of her daughter's marriage to Finchly, she writes that she "will not embitter the present moment of joy by denying [her] pardon and blessing." When Finchly leaves Victoria pregnant and alone, her mother and sister go to stay with her. Her circle of sympathetic friends share the idea that all women should stand by one another, an idea repeated in the subplots. "I am sorry that you or any other woman should rejoice in the fall of our own Sex," one character reprimands a gossip-monger. ". . . Ought we not rather to . . . shield her reputation, remembering that errors or vice in one woman reflect on all of the sex?"[6] To forgive a woman who bore a child out of wedlock ran contrary to social custom, but Haswell valued every woman and hoped that redemption could follow forgiveness. The convention of the novel required that her guilty heroine die despite the fact that she had believed herself married and despite the love of family and friends. But Haswell clearly thought that readers should forgive and assist those whom society condemned.

Forgiveness constituted only part of the support and guidance that Haswell believed women should offer one another, and she demonstrates several times in the novel the necessity for a community of women. When Finchly's deceit becomes known and Victoria bears her bastard child and grows insane, she is surrounded by a group of sympathetic women who do everything in their power to protect her, uniting in their condemnation of the evil seducer. The support and guidance offered by a circle of women friends could seem all the more essential in view of society's double standard. Haswell illustrates that double standard when she portrays Lord Selton's tacit acceptance of Harry Finchly's duplicity. Though Lord Selton is a good man, worthy of marriage to one of the heroines of the novel, he lifts not a finger to warn Victoria or her family of the compromising position in which Harry Finchly is placing the unwary girl. Even some women revile the character of a woman taken in by a deceitful man. Victoria protests that the sexual crimes of women are never forgiven, though men go unpunished for the same acts:

The world will never pardon us; while men may plunge in every idle vice and yet be received in all companies, and too often caressed by the brave and worthy. Can you tell me why this is, Bell? Are crimes less so when committed by men than by women? (1:131–32)

But neither Bell nor anyone else in Victoria's circle has an answer. The only solution Haswell can offer, unsatisfactory though it seems, is for women to protect themselves as best they can. "Since so fair and unspotted, nature formed us, it is our duty to preserve as much as possible the brightness of our soul, and render it pure and holy to the hands of Him that gave it" (1:132–33). Such passivity seems the reasonable approach, considering the social structure that holds to one standard for men and another for women.

Although she would like to see women exercise mutual assistance, Haswell does not unrealistically idealize women. She portrays in *Victoria* a full gamut of female characters, including one unequivocal villain. Lady Maskwell has no redeeming virtues; she lies and cheats to obtain the position and money she seeks, and she permits no lover or family connection to stand between her and her ambition. She turns penitent only after she has lost everything to a male partner even more unscrupulous than she is, and she spends the rest of her life in humble obscurity only, the reader feels, because she has grown too old and lacks the resources to start a new life of crime. Lady Maskwell thus becomes the first of Rowson's line of female villains who include Lassonia in *The Inquisitor*, the Jamaican wife in *Mary; or, The Test of Honour*, and LaRue in *Charlotte, A Tale of Truth*.

The social ill that annoys Haswell most is the bias in favor of social rank and wealth, practiced by both men and women. Haswell believed that virtue knows no class distinction and that people earn respect according to their actions, not their names. But she also admitted the importance placed upon social class. Victoria's faith in romantic love clashes with social reality, as neither her lover nor his parents consider her humble rank adequate for marriage into the family of Finchlys. Haswell was not so romantic as to believe that love conquers all, and she taught in *Victoria*, as she would in *The Inquisitor*, that a woman can best handle herself in the world when she has full understanding of its ways.

Another social evil that Haswell deplores in *Victoria* is the emphasis on a woman's appearance. All of her admirable characters dress plainly, and she derides the worship of youth and beauty:

Ye virgins and matrons whoe'er felt the pow'r, Of M——'s cosmetics, come round and adore, For the widow of sixty, and nymph of sixteen, Both alike with a blooming complexion are seen, And all must be lovely whose cheeks still discloses Like nature's fair bloom, M——'s bloom of Roses. (2:106)

Haswell satirizes the aging Lady Winterly, who dresses and talks and giggles like an adolescent, and she also dispels the notion that a young woman can rely solely on her looks to fulfill her needs and aims.

In keeping with this unromantic view of society Haswell also satirizes some aspects of the sentimental literary tradition. The epistolary style with multiple points of view permits her to include some characters who behave sentimentally and some who do not. Bell Hartley, an intelligent and virtuous woman, rejects a marriage proposal from an honest, wealthy, and good man in defiance of her friends' advice. "I must have a little flirtation first," protests the lively Bell. "Consider I am just come to town, and do you suppose I will become a strange, grave, domestic animal called a wife already?" When Bell finally marries, she refuses to view marriage in conventional sentimental terms. "Poor Bell Hartley," she writes of herself. "Thou art now no more! dear days of liberty, thou art gone, and all my future years are to be spent in vowed obedience" (I, 159). She cannot bear to describe her own wedding, which would require a sentimentality she simply does not own, for, she confesses, she neither cried nor fainted. Furthermore, she plans to fight occasionally with her husband, on the grounds that too much domestic bliss promotes dullness.

Underlying all these themes of filial piety, seduction, forgiveness for the "fallen" woman, the community of women, and the emptiness of the social world is the idea that women must curb their passions and exercise their reason:

The first step toward (happiness), is teaching our passions to be submissive to the rules of reason. (1:182)

The turbulence of passion, if not timely curbed by reason, will corrupt even virtues, and bring [one] acquainted with nothing but vice. (2:22–23)

Over the years Rowson maintained this conviction and expressed it in various forms. Some twenty years later she wrote a song which asked "Where Can Peace of Mind Be Found?" Her answer: "Where reason sheds her sober ray, where virtue's laws the passions bind, where faith and virtue stay." But in *Victoria* the author had not yet fully developed a reasonable and self-sufficient heroine. In later novels Rowson was to develop a heroine who could withstand both the temptations of seduction and the blasts of gossip and succeed by means of her own reason and virtue.

Victoria was reviewed in the London *Monthly Review* of January, 1787, and in the *Critical Review* of the same month. The *Critical Review* refused to criticize a novel that aimed to teach filial piety. The author "has executed her design in a number of well-chosen pathetic tales," the reviewer wrote. "On such a cause Criticism smooths his brow, and takes off his spectacles, willing to see no fault. She who would support the cause of piety and virtue cannot err."[7] The *Monthly Review* showed less tolerance, faulting the novel for its lack of originality though still considering the book a worthwhile first effort.[8] The novel was issued in a second edition in 1790, but no known copy of this edition exists. Although *Victoria* was never published in America, it was widely sold. Between 1789 and 1816 at least ten American booksellers stocked the novel in Boston, Salem, Newburyport, and New York.[9]

The Inquisitor

Two years later Rowson published her second novel, *The Inquisitor*, a loosely structured, picaresque series of short stories or scenes related by a narrator. Rowson chose a male narrator, she wrote in the preface, for the sake of decorum. "A man can go places with propriety that a woman cannot." This narrator, a kindly gentleman, obtains a ring that renders him invisible at will, enabling him to enter into situations whereby he can help the poor and vulnerable. Some of the scenes are linked by the same characters, but others are isolated scenes which the magically endowed narrator happens upon. Women commonly did not write in this picaresque form, but Rowson feminized the genre by using the concerns of the domestic novel as primary subjects for her narrator's adventures. The narrator avoids the male domains of business and politics to deal only with the narrow world of women: unpaid debts to a grocer, a deceptive suitor, an attempted seduction. Rowson handled these quick-paced brief scenes well, and she interspersed among the stories several short essays.

The preface to *The Inquisitor* attests to a lightness of purpose not found in Rowson's other novels. "I will honestly confess that this work was written solely for my amusement," she wrote. Most women authors of Rowson's day professed a more serious intent in their prefaces, claiming a desperate need for money to support their children or at least a somber didactic aim that allowed no "amusement." Rowson downplayed what in fact were serious intentions, for *The Inquisitor* was by no means a frivolous work. It conveyed her views of contemporary fiction, her concerns with women, her moral didacticism, and her views on Christianity.

In one sense Rowson sought to place herself in the sentimental tradition. She stated in her preface that *The Inquisitor* was a conscious but humble imitation of Laurence Sterne, by which she meant Sterne's *Sentimental Journey Through France and Italy* (1768). Rowson to some extent modeled her novel's style and content after this work that she admired. Stylistically she imitated Sterne's frequent use of dashes. In the plot she imitated Sterne's narrator, a man of feeling, who moves from one incident to another. Her narrator, like Sterne's, displays his "feeling" in his ability to be moved by the emotions of others. Unlike Henry Mackenzie's *Man of Feeling* (1771), the purest example of this sentimental hero, Rowson's narrator is not merely a tenderhearted and gullible innocent who indulges in emotion for its own sake. Like the Sternean narrator, Rowson's man of feeling displays his sensibility in acts of generosity and Christian charity. He gives to the poor, rescues maidens from seduction, and lectures the selfish and unfeeling. As a sentimental hero, he dislikes the ways of the world, but he understands them and tries to effect actual good.

Rowson's belief in the didactic function of fiction limited her imitation of sentimentality. She satirized in *The Inquisitor* some aspects of the sentimental tradition that countered her views about the purpose of the novel. She intensely disliked the standard sentimental, romantic, and unrealistic plots which, as most contemporary critics of fiction argued, could too easily turn the heads of young women readers. But she knew the literary marketplace, so her narrator recommends to an aspiring novelist a sentimental plot with an unrealistic heroine whose long-suffering virtue finally earns her the reward of marriage to her true love. Rowson disapproved of such fiction because women readers whose knowledge of the world was confined almost exclusively to the home might confuse romanticism with reality. Another passage in *The Inquisitor* makes clear how this could happen:

Love! cries the lovely girl, whose imagination is warmed by the perusal of a sentimental novel . . . Give me love and Strephon, an humble cottage shaded with woodbine; for love will render the retreat delightful!

Charmed with the enchanting scene her busy fancy draws, she imagines happiness exists only in a cottage; and that for love of her dear Strephon, she could easily, and without regret forego all the undulgencies [*sic*] of her father's house; all the advantages of wealth, and solace herself with a brown crust and a pitcher of milk . . . and without a moment's deliberation, throws herself upon the honor of a man, who perhaps, had no further regard for her than the hope of sharing her fortune might excite.[10]

In her own fiction Rowson employs aspects of the sentimental tradition but carefully avoids an unrealistically romantic plot.

Consistent with her didactic view of fiction, Rowson's second complaint about contemporary fiction was its emphasis upon emotion rather than reason. She particularly disliked the work of a novelist like Henri Rousseau, whose *Julie, ou la nouvelle Heloise* (1761) contained a hero and heroine guided by sentiment alone.

The Inquisitor's tale of Annie, born to affluence and educated on sentimental authors, conveys Rowson's views of Rousseau. Annie has lost her financial independence and is supporting herself as a milliner's assistant when she falls prey to Mr. Winlove, an irreligious man who pretends "to laugh at all obligations, moral and religious." Mr. Winlove uses Rousseau and Charles Churchill to seduce the unfortunate Annie.

Take example, dear Annie, said he, from the excellent *Eloise* of Rousseau.
She had never read it.
He recommended it very strongly for her perusal.
As she returned home, passing a library, Mr. Winlove purchased the pernicious novel, and gave it to Annie.
She took it home—and read it—her judgment was perverted—she believed in the reality of a platonic passion—she thought she had the virtue of an Eloise, and Mr. Winlove the honour of a St. Preux.
Churchill was the next author that was recommended.
She read—she listened to the soft language of love, and imbibed pernicious poison from every page she read, and every word she heard.
Trusting to her own strength and virtue, she made a private assignation— met him—confessed she loved—and was lost.
. . . . Her reputation stained—without peace—despised and insulted by her own sex, pitied by the other, and renounced by her uncle, who had bound her apprentice, she became the associate of the abandoned and profligate; and reduced to chuse [*sic*] the dreadful alternative of death or infamy, became a partner in vices which once she would have shuddered to think on. (3:172–73)

With comic abruptness Rowson thus exaggerated the effect of a book, though the exaggeration does not disguise her belief that women should be guided by reason rather than emotion, a conviction further demonstrated by her later novels.

More than any of Rowson's other books, *The Inquisitor* also deals with her concern for the woman as artist. Drawing from her own experience, she showed two kinds of problems facing the woman artist. The morality of plagiarism is depicted in a scene in which a young woman takes her manuscript to "Mr. C——ke, bookseller." This unpleasant character recommends that the young woman not bother writing original fiction but copy her stories from magazines and offer them to the public as new work. Worse, he recommends she write "a story full of intrigue, wrote with levity, and tending to convey loose ideas." Rowson knew that many people did not believe women should write for publication, so she felt that women who did so must exercise particular care not to offend by dishonesty or any lack of integrity. She refused to listen to Cooke's advice and never took another manuscript to him. In *The Inquisitor* she has her young woman author refuse to deal in any way with this unscrupulous businessman, reflecting the woman's moral superiority. Though Rowson never shared the idea that women had a finer moral nature than men, she did consistently make her "good" women characters morally upright so that they set examples for her readers.

A second problem peculiar to the woman artist as Rowson saw her was public disapproval, especially from other women. Rowson described a young poet, Ellen, whose efforts to establish her career are thwarted by a Mrs. Greenham, who ridicules the aspiring poet as unladylike. "I am sure women have no business with pens in their hands," Mrs. Greenham protests. "They had better mend their cloaths, and look after the family (2:143–44). But Ellen finds a defender in an old gentleman who believes writing is a worthwhile occupation for women and finds writers to be good, moral women:

Why may not a woman, if she has leisure and genius, take up her pen to gratify both herself and friends. I am not ashamed to acknowledge that I have perused the productions of some of our female pens, with the highest satisfactions; and am happy when I find any woman has so large a fund of amusement in her own mind. I never heard of a woman, who was fond of her pen, complain of the tediousness of time; nor, did I ever know such a woman extravagantly fond of dress, public amusements, or expensive gaiety; yet, I have seen many women of genius prove themselves excellent mothers, wives, and daughters. (2:144)

Rowson was sensitive to criticism of women authors and actors all her life though she never let such criticism deter her from writing or performing.

Related to this criticism from women is Rowson's regret that women so seldom value the friendship of their own sex. Like modern feminists, she held that women needed the support they could find in close relationships with friends of their own sex, and she demonstrated the importance of a close community of women friends in other, later fiction.

Rowson used the loose structure of *The Inquisitor* to range freely among other moral and didactic subjects, again consistent with her view of fiction. One short chapter, for example, contains an essay attacking the "modern man of honour" who will have his pleasures whether or not he can afford to pay for them. Another, entitled "The Lounger," depicts a young loafer who neither reads nor thinks but whiles away his time in bored idleness. Women too come in for their share of social criticism. The chapter on "The Actress" contains a lesson on the democracy of virtue, a favorite theme repeated in later Rowson works. Here an actress receives censure for feeling too proud to speak to a mere barber. "Virtue begets respect wherever she appears," Rowson's narrator advises. Since goodness respects no class boundaries, it need not always accompany wealth or title but can and should appear in all classes and occupations.

Finally, Rowson included in *The Inquisitor* some of her views on Christianity, views which reflected both her moral concerns and her rationality. She believed that Christianity should be reflected in behaviour, not in mere ceremony:

The christian [*sic*] religion, requires neither bulls, nor goats for offerings; neither gold nor embroidery for the decoration of their temples; neither precious stones, or golden ornaments for their priests' vestments. Its sacrifice is a contrite heart; its incense is a meek and quiet spirit; its richest pillars and best ornaments are faith in the Redeemer's blood; and that charity which at once enlargeth the heart, and openeth the hand; and that love to God which envinces itself in purity of life in sincerity, humility, and grateful obedience. (1:217)

This perspective remained essentially unchanged through Rowson's life. Though a staunch Protestant who distrusted Catholicism, she always refused to ally herself with any one church. She believed genuine religion depended not on ritual but on simple goodness of heart. That belief did not, however, lead her, as it did later women, to associate religion with sentiment and sympathetic tears. Her faith was founded on reason and understanding of the Scriptures, for her approach to religion, as to the rest of her life, was essentially rational.

The Inquisitor at once looked back to Rowson's experiences as a child and young woman and forward to some themes she would develop in later writings. For instance, in *The Inquisitor* Rowson describes a young woman seeking employment as governess. The character's description of her background clearly echoes Susanna Haswell's life. This and other sketches, such as the one about "Mr. C——ke, bookseller," suggest that Rowson borrowed from her own experiences for parts of this book. At the same time she repeated some of the themes she had introduced in *Victoria* and would use again and again in her later novels and plays, including the virtues of filial piety and forgiveness for the "fallen woman." She also introduced new themes that would reappear in later works, specifically, parental guidance in children's education, and the uselessness of boarding-school accomplishments for young ladies.

The Inquisitor was reviewed in June, 1788, in the *Critical Review* and in August that year by the *Monthly Review*. The reviews for this second novel were as brief as they had been for *Victoria*, short paragraphs which offered no serious analysis or even plot summary. The *Critical Review* found that the novel more closely resembled *The Rambles of Frankly* by Elizabeth Bonhote than the works of Laurence Sterne but objected strongly to the device of the narrator's ring, which the reviewer called "a trick so artificial, as at once to disgust the more rational reader." However, the reviewer conceded, "there are many pathetic traits which speak to the heart, and are drawn from nature: they are extremely affecting, when we forget the ring." The *Monthly Review* found "nothing of novelty in the idea nor any thing particularly striking in the execution of the work," but it approved of the novel for young readers and commended the author for her "feeling heart."[11]

With these reviews of her second novel, Rowson by now realized what other women novelists had already learned, that critics did not consider women writers worthy of serious critical review. While the editors of the *Critical* and *Monthly Reviews* nobly tried to review almost every book printed, they believed women writers should be held to different standards than men; women, they thought, wrote exclusively for women and children, so their books need only teach morality and tell a reasonably interesting story. When they spoke of "correctness of style" in a woman's work, they usually meant only spelling and grammar. A book by a woman sufficed if it would do no harm. Reviews of her first two books, however, by no means diminished Rowson's enthusiasm for the art of writing novels. Satisfied if she wrote acceptably for "youthful friends," she did not concern herself with literary style, and she happily sacrificed narrative consistency for the sake of didactic intent.

Mary; or, the Test of Honour

As soon as *The Inquisitor* was sold, Rowson began work on her next novel, *Mary; or, The Test of Honour*, published the following year (1789). For the first time she published the book anonymously, like most women's novels of the day. More than any other of her works to date *The Test of Honour* seems to have been written for money, and in fact Samuel Lorenzo Knapp, the nineteenth-century writer who knew her, states that Rowson merely reworked this novel from material she obtained from a publisher. She obviously felt willing to lower her standards when she needed money, but she did not sign her name to the book, and she never acknowledged it.[12] The publisher and probable source of the original material was John Abraham, who ran a circulating library in St. Swithin's Lane, Lombard Street. A circulating library rented books at three pence a day, or by quarterly or annual subscriptions, to those who could not afford the five shilling purchase price of a two-volume novel. Rowson designed *The Test of Honour* to appeal to the lower-middle class ladies who patronized these libraries. The stock characters behave predictably; the standard sentimental domestic plot is enlarged to include both sea adventure and a captivity narrative; and the didacticism of the story is supplemented by a digression on the education of young people.

Despite her previous publications, Rowson posed in the preface as a new author. Adopting the modest tone characteristic of women authors, she anticipated criticism from matrons who might tell her she had better employ her time at her needle:

If I use my pen for amusement, if I never neglect more material concerns, to follow that amusement; why may I not indulge a propensity, so innocent in itself, and which I shall take care shall never be productive of any harm to others?[13]

Elsewhere in the preface to *The Inquisitor* Rowson insisted that she had written that novel for her own entertainment. But the lightness of tone in that preface was now replaced by a more defensive stance, though she still maintained her right to create for her own amusement.

Although Rowson did not claim any truth to her story, she asked her readers to remember that her heroine was not merely a child of fiction:

[She is an] amiable woman who, taking reason and religion for the guide of all her actions, keeping her passions under due controul [sic] sunk not beneath the pressure of adversity; but, supported by that Providence who delights in virtue, passed through life with honour and applause. (Preface)

This defense of her heroine maintains the view of fiction articulated in *The Inquisitor*, that is, that fiction is acceptable if didactic and not excessively sentimental. Rowson also displayed in the preface the pride that characterized her attitude toward all her work:

I offer no apology, nor alledge [sic] any particular reason for suffering these sheets to be printed; for it ever appeared a ridiculous thing to me, for a person to apologize for a fault (if a fault it is deemed, sage critics), which they can neither recall nor correct. (Preface)

Obsequious apologies frequently prefaced women's novels, but Rowson refused to lie for the sake of convention. Nor would she offer any reasons for "commencing author" that might "gratify the curiosity of impertinent, ignorant people." She trusted, she said, that the "well-bred, sensible reader" would not trouble to ask such a thing.

The Test of Honour follows the adventures of Mary Newton from childhood, when she is orphaned, to her marriage perhaps fifteen years later. Mary stays first with one guardian, and then with another. She falls in love with young Frederick Stephens but refuses to pursue him because he is far more wealthy and of a higher station than she. When she learns of a bequest from a rich uncle in Jamaica, she sails for the island and by happy accident discovers herself on the same boat as Frederick. Their voyage is interrupted by a violent storm, which destroys their boat and casts Mary and Frederick, the sole survivors, on a deserted island. There they live in chaste harmony and without any hardship whatever until rescued. Once again bound for Jamaica, their ship is intercepted first by Spanish pirates and then by Algerians, who take Frederick prisoner. Mary finally arrives in Jamaica only to discover her uncle has died and an unscrupulous cousin has usurped her inheritance. She returns to England and brings suit to recover her fortune. Once she acquires the wealth that is her due, she feels free to marry Frederick, who conveniently escapes from the Algerians in order to oblige her.

Subplots include the story of Emily Elwin, who commits adultery and dies in punishment, and Caroline Watson, an orphan who works as a tavernmaid until discovered accidentally by a long-lost and of course rich uncle. But a more interesting subplot to the reader acquainted with Rowson is the story of Semira the fair Greek, a story later adapted for the play *Slaves in Algiers*. Semira and her sister Eumenia have been made slaves of the Moorish sultan, Hali, who has also purchased Frederick Stephens. The girls' father has tried unsuccessfully to free his daughters and finally travels to Algeria hoping to effect their escape, but he too succumbs to the clever Moor and is made prisoner. Semira, more resourceful than the men in the story, enlists the help of Frederick and contrives an elaborate escape plan, but that too is thwarted. Finally, in desperation Semira decides to sacrifice herself in order to save her sister, her father, and Frederick. In exchange for a solemn promise that her loved ones will be set free, she marries Hali and converts to Mohammedanism. Of course she has no intention of sacrificing her virginity to such a pagan, but before she can plunge a dagger into her breast, Hali is so impressed by the nobility of her sacrifice that he agrees to annul the marriage and set Semira free with the others. All the stories in *The Test of Honour* thus amply demonstrate the rewards of virtue, but this subplot provides a striking example of filial piety and female fortitude.

As these plot summaries suggest, the plot structure in *A Test of Honour* is weakened by improbabilities. Unlikely if not impossible events occur with frequency in both the main plot line as well as the subplots. In structure the book lacks the coherence of other Rowson novels, as the plot and subplots are interwoven ineffectively so as to interrupt one another and sometimes confuse the reader. The subplot concerning Caroline Watson, for instance, is inserted inappropriately at a crucial point in the relation of the main story, and the resolution of two subplots delays the ending of the novel for some sixty pages after the climax of the main plot line. Such structural weaknesses are atypical of Rowson's other novels.

Another weakness of this novel is that its characterization is flat and often predictable. The character of Mary is made bearable, at least for a modern reader, only by her resemblance to some other Rowson heroines. Typically, she is a young woman thrown on her own devices. Despite her unflagging conventionality, she asserts an independence echoed repeatedly in other works by Rowson:

You will see that I am a free born English woman, and that I have spirit enough to assert those rights which nature and my country allow me, while my actions are innocent, and my wishes guided by prudence and virtue, I shall think no person has a right to assume a tyrannical sway over me. (1:34)

This speech unfortunately is one of the liveliest in the book, for the dialogue more often consists of set speeches and trite phrases that closely resemble other fictional works of the time.

Another similarity between Mary and other Rowson heroines is her acquaintance with the ways of the world. When confronted by a dishonest ship captain, for instance, she knows how to handle him. "I will pay you before these men," she tells him, "and then you cannot pretend to deny receiving the money." She also demands a receipt. And finally, Mary resembles other Rowson heroines in her sense of adventure. To acquire the inheritance that will render her independent, she undertakes a sea voyage with only a paid companion. Though she suffers shipwreck followed by a Robinson Crusoe existence on a desert island, she does not give up but, as soon as she is rescued, continues to make her way to Jamaica. Instead of meekly accepting the loss of her inheritance, she returns home where she can bring suit against her dishonest cousin. As reward for her troubles, she in the end finds a loving husband, wealth, and happiness.

Such adventures distinguish *The Test of Honour* from the conventional domestic novel, but the book still retains the trappings of sentimentality. In fact, a reader cannot but wonder if the author merely left intact long passages from whatever original material she used as basis for the novel, for many descriptions such as this one seem tinged with parody: "The saffron-robed Aurora had just begun to chase the fading stars, and with her dewy fingers increase the fragrance of the opening flowers." A lady lies down with "the drop of sensibility bedewing her pillow," and even the heroine who can defy her would-be jailors and instigate a lawsuit succumbs to frequent swoons. Such purple passages do not seem the work of the Susanna Rowson whose theory of fiction precluded sentimentality. A novel had to convey reality, she believed, in order to instruct and set an example for its young readers. *The Test of Honour* fails in part because its combination of sentimentality and realism produces an inconsistent picture of women.

Consistent with the sentimental tradition, women in *The Test of Honour* are described as soft and tractable, for "nature formed them friendly, affectionate, noble, and unsuspicious"; but Mary survives her rather masculine adventures only because she becomes distrustful and defensive of her rights.

The Test of Honour takes up several of Rowson's favorite didactic themes. Filial piety, the theme introduced in *Victoria* and repeated in *The Inquisitor*, is portrayed both in the subplots and in the main plot as essential for marital happiness. Emily Elwin and Harry Fentum, for instance, marry in defiance of his parents and suffer an ill-fated relationship. Mary, on the other hand, refuses her lover's proposals until his father gives his blessing. When her lover offers eternal love and a life in a "humble cottage" because he will lose his inheritance for marrying her, Mary chides his "romantic fantasy," pointing out that such a life could lead only to "care, chagrin, and disappointment." The theme of sympathy for the fallen woman, also used in the two previous novels, occurs in the subplot involving Emily Elwin. Mary finds Emily begging on the streets and takes her in, regardless of her adultery. And Rowson's theme of the virtue found among the middle classes surfaces in social criticism. Frederick Stephens's father, an old misogynist, refuses to allow his son to wed Mary because she is merely a farmer's daughter. He prefers to match his son to an heiress. In the end, however, Mary's virtues persuade the elder Mr. Fentum that she indeed deserves his son and teaches him that even women can be "generous."

Another idea in *The Test of Honour* repeated in later novels is that education for girls should be practical. Rowson condemned girls' boarding schools that taught useless accomplishments. Mary's guardian first sent her to a boarding school:

[There] every method was taken to counteract and undermine the excellent precepts and solid virtues her mother had so ardently laboured to inculcate. She learnt to jabber bad French, and sing worse Italian; the more essential branches of needlework were neglected, that she might learn embroidery, clothwork, and fifty other things, equally useless; drawing, or rather scrawling, was not forgot; and to dance with ease and elegance, was a thing of the greatest consequence. (52)

Although girls' boarding schools grew increasingly popular with the English middle classes during the late eighteenth century, such schools were held to no standards beyond those set by the headmistress, who might be anyone who deemed herself sufficiently educated to supervise the education of others. Rowson was not alone in her attack on these schools. In 1809 the novelist and teacher Helena Wells criticized boarding schools she had visited before the turn of the century, citing their unqualified teachers and lazy, uninformed headmistresses. She too attacked the practice of educating the daughters of tradesmen in "useless accomplishments" when they needed practical domestic arts.[14] Rowson continued to criticize contemporary women's education until she was herself able to open a school and implement her theories.

The reviews of *The Test of Honour* might have caused a less-determined woman to seek another vocation. The *Critical Review* dismissed the novel as "trifling," the work of an inexperienced writer.[15] The *Monthly Review* refused to give the novel serious consideration and also assumed that it was the writer's first attempt.[16] To prepare herself for criticism, Rowson had anticipated in the preface to this novel that "the venerable society of reviewers" would, in a line from Shakespeare, "report me as they find me, / Nothing extenuate, nor set down aught / in malice." As for their criticism of her plot and characters, she denied any concern. She had at this time little interest in style or form except as they appealed to her audience. *The Test of Honour*, flawed as it was, accomplished for Rowson what many novels were doing for other women at the time: it paid its author for her labors,[17] it entertained, and it instructed. And just now, novels were Rowson's only outlet for teaching.

Mentoria

In 1791 Rowson published her fourth work of fiction, *Mentoria; or, The Young Lady's Friend.* Her preface to this work sounded characteristically straightforward. "A good book needs no preface," she maintained, but she found herself obliged to write one nonetheless. "If I leave one out I'm inferring it's a good book and will be considered conceited. If I write a preface and confess the book's faults, I prepossess readers against it."[18] She prefaced her book, therefore, with a statement of purpose, her desire to help other women:

My design was . . . an anxious desire to see all my dear countrywomen as truly amiable as they are universally acknowledged to be beautiful; it was a wish to convince them that true happiness can never be met within the temple of dissipation and folly; she . . . dwells only in the heart conscious of performing its duty, and is the constant companion of those, who, content with the station in which it has pleased Providence to place them entirely free from envy or malice. (ii)

This theme of contentment with one's station in life unifies the various stories throughout the book, and its unrelieved didacticism suggests that Rowson sought to atone for having written *Mary; or, the Test of Honour* for money.

Although too proud to apologize for her efforts, Rowson did feel self-conscious about her lack of education, and she anticipated harsh judgment by male critics:

I must also be judged by some sage critic 'who with spectacles on nose, and pouch by's side,' with lengthened visage and contemptuous smile, sits down to review the literary productions of a *woman*. He turns over a few pages, and then

> catching the Author at some that or therefore,
> at once *condemns* her without why or wherefore.

Then alas! what may not be my fate? whose education was necessarily circumscribed, whose little knowledge has been simply gleaned from pure nature, and who, on a subject of such importance, write as I feel, with enthusiasm. (iii–iv)

The unfavorable reviews of her other works had made her self-conscious, but Rowson simply attributed faults in her writing to her inadequate education, the inevitable fate of woman. She took comfort in the "purity" of her intentions for which critics could never fault her, and she left it to those "who have received a liberal education, to write with that taste and elegance which can only be acquired by a thorough knowledge of the classics" (iv). In actual fact, Rowson longed for a better education and continued her self-education all her life.

In structure *Mentoria* more closely resembles *The Inquisitor* than any of Rowson's other novels, though it is not a picaresque work. It is a collection of ten letters, three short stories, and one essay, compiled, the author says in a footnote, for women who do not read novels. The book opens with verses "addressed to a Young Lady on her leaving school" (a poem included in *Victoria* under the title "To Anna"). The title-character is the letter writer, a female mentor, Helena Askam, who has served as governess to the four Winworth daughters. Now that the girls have moved to London, their governess writes them letters signed "Mentoria." The book opens with a six-page biography of Mentoria, so impersonally related that it reads like a "character" or compilation of abilities and attributes. The letters usually begin with an account of what Mentoria has heard of the young ladies' behavior, a short sermon on how they ought to behave, followed by a brief narrative for illustration. The tone of the letters is friendly but firm, for Mentoria will permit no deviation from the conduct she considers essential for one girls' reputation and happiness. "You must early learn to submit, without murmuring to the will of your father," she admonishes in the first letter, and the others are equally rigid in their recommendation of choice of friends, dependence upon reliable women friends, and pieces of advice. These letters constitute slightly less than half the book.

The story of "Lydia and Marian" is inserted between letters VI and VII without explanation. This lengthy short story fictionalizes some of the doctrines of the letters. The main point reasserts the idea that young women should not aspire to a class above their own, a lesson illustrated through two generations. Both the mother, Dorcas, and years later the daughter, Marian, are seduced by young noblemen who promise to marry them but leave after fake or illegal marriages. The story ends happily after the second generation has learned the lesson. In addition to its moral, the story is remarkable for its unusual style. Unlike Rowson's previous fiction, the dialogue is presented without quotation marks. The narration moves quickly and is related in an almost childlike way. Rowson may have borrowed this tale from an old source, for it seems almost archetypal in its presentation. Witness this description by the young Marian of her future seducer: ". . . he only wanted to kiss me, and I ran away from him. But he was so handsome, and he had such a pretty thing to ride in; dear, dear, how I should like to ride in such an one" (80).

The last of Mentoria's letters is written to Gertrude Winworth after the birth of her daughter, and it contains some of Rowson's infrequent advice on raising children. Like a modern feminist, Rowson rejected the emphasis on romance and marriage that parents give girls but not boys. Ahead of her time, Rowson realized that when girls are repeatedly reminded of marriage as their only destiny, they achieve nothing else:

There is one thing which parents are very apt, not only to themselves, but to suffer their servants to do the same; that is, when any little' master visits at the house, nearly of miss's age, she is told that he is her little husband, and that she must hold up her head, and behave like a woman, or she will never be married.

Thus is the idea of love and lovers introduced into their little hearts. This is, to me, the most foolish conduct in the world. . . . Teach them the difference between right and wrong, and convince their reason, by pointing out the real way to promote their own happiness. (240–41)

This same idea appeared later in the poem "Women as They Are" contained in *Miscellaneous Poems*. Only after she opened her own school could Rowson apply this theory, and her later textbooks reflect her continued belief in young women's need to think about the world in an unromantic and selfless way. Despite the soundness of her thinking about young children, Rowson took relatively little interest in them. She seldom included them in her fiction and directed most of her pedagogical efforts toward the education of young women.

For herself, as a woman with no domestic aspirations, Rowson preferred a classical education. Most women of the middle class, however, were destined to spend their lives as household managers and so needed to know how to budget, make and mend clothes, and cook; and it was these women Rowson hoped to assist. She tried in her fiction to persuade women of the need for these skills, without which they would be too uneducated to perform their life's work. The pretensions of the expanding middle class had produced many wives ill prepared for their domestic responsibilities, and this problem came increasingly to be noticed by nineteenth-century women's magazines.[19] Criticism of women disturbed Rowson, who believed that encouragement and education could eradicate the causes of such criticism.

Following the essay on female education are two stories, "Urganda and Fatima" and "The Incendiary," both of which, according to the author's footnote, had appeared earlier in magazines. "Urganda and Fatima" continues the theme of the false allure of social ambition. The peasant Fatima dreams of the glory of the court until the fairy

Urganda transforms her into the favorite consort of the emperor, and Fatima quickly learns that her real happiness lies in her humble home. The tale offers but a slight variation on an old fable which Rowson told with simplicity. The tone of the fable contrasts sharply with the final story, "The Incendiary," which reveals two sordid London scenes.[20]

Rowson wrote *Mentoria* as an experiment in a genre other than pure fiction. The book resembles the female courtesy book such as Eliza Haywood's *Female Spectator* (1744–46), which combined essays, fanciful stories, and epistolary apologues to instruct women on subjects of interest to them. Yet *Mentoria* seems strangely disjointed. The book reiterates Rowson's favorite themes of filial piety, the importance of female friendships, and so on, but these are woven into moral fables within straightforward epistolary essays, and this heavily didactic format lacks the interest of the novels.

Rowson took *Mentoria* to William Lane at the Minerva Press in Leadenhall Street. Possibly she sold the manuscripts of both *Charlotte* and *Mentoria* together, for William Lane frequently purchased manuscripts in lots.[21] Rowson's choice of William Lane suggests her increased sense of purpose. She was no longer writing merely for the few pounds a manuscript would bring but rather as a means of contributing to the education of other women. Her own experiences since she had returned to England had convinced her that many middle-class women lived unhappy and unproductive lives, and she wanted, through education, to improve their situation. She could reach a wide audience through circulating libraries, which offered a growing reading public an inexpensive access to books. William Lane would put Susanna Rowson into those libraries. He had been publishing successfully for fifteen years but only six years ago had turned to publication of novels. Using a surprisingly modern technique, he had first created a market by traveling around England organizing libraries and then returning to London to supply this self-created demand. Rowson had seen Lane's large statue of Minerva with plumed helmet and Grecian draperies erected over the door in Leadenhall Street the previous year, and she had finally decided to trust her manuscripts to him. Though Lane had a reputation for tight-fistedness, he usually paid a novelist between ten and twenty pounds for the copyright and then in the usual practice kept all proceeds himself.[22] If he anticipated a book's success, he issued it bound in boards, but most novels, like *Mentoria*, he merely sewed together. Copies of the first edition of *Mentoria* sold for three shillings each.[23]

This first edition contained on an unnumbered page at the end an advertisement: "Just published. Charlotte: or a tale of truth. In 2 Vols. 12 mo.—Price 5s. sewed." Following this announcement was a review of *Charlotte* taken from the *Critical Review* of April, 1791. Quite possibly Rowson sold the two manuscripts to Lane at the same time, and he issued *Charlotte* first. A copy of the 1791 edition of *Mentoria* is located today in the New York Public library. A second edition was published in Dublin in the same year, but whether this was because the Irish booksellers who ordered it recognized Rowson's name, and purchased it from Lane properly, or merely pirated the book is not known.[24] One American edition appeared in Philadelphia in 1794, printed by Samuel Harrison Smith for Robert Campbell. The book was imported into Boston in 1793 and was listed in the catalogs of at least fourteen other booksellers from 1797 to 1891 in Albany, Boston, New York, Philadelphia, and Worcester.[25] No reviews of the book either in England or the United States have been located.

Charlotte: A Tale of Truth

In the same year that she published *Mentoria* Rowson published the novel that would later become America's first best-seller. She took this manuscript to William Lane, who published *Charlotte: A Tale of Truth* in large type in order to fill the conventional two volumes. (The only known copy of this 1791 edition is located in the Barrett Collection at the University of Virginia.) William Lane chose this novel in which to present his plan for a "literary museum, or novel repository" of manuscripts that would "entertain or improve the mind, elucidate the sciences, or be of any utility." He promised printing "with expedition, correctness, accuracy and elegance" on good paper. He refused to print anything unless it was "founded on the basis of Virtue." He printed this advertisement in *Charlotte* to reach other writers who wanted to begin as Rowson had begun, writing for patrons of circulating libraries whose shelves Lane could so profitably stock.

Lane apparently expected better sales from *Charlotte* than from *Mentoria*, for he issued it at two prices, 2/6 and 3 shillings, the first probably for the sewn volumes and the second for volumes bound in

boards. But *Charlotte* did not sell in England as it was to sell in the
United States. Although the *Critical Review* evaluated it favorably,
finding the story sufficiently realistic to be authentic,[26] no second edition appeared until 1819.[27] Rowson had to wait for the first American
edition of her book in 1794 to learn that she had written a novel that
would bring her fame.

The plot of *Charlotte: A Tale of Truth* is simple. Charlotte, a fifteen-
year-old girl in a Chichester boarding school, is persuaded by her dis-
solute French teacher, Mademoiselle LaRue, to run away to America
with a dashing young army officer, Lieutenant Montraville. Once in
New York, Montraville ignores his promise to marry Charlotte and
soon falls in love with the beautiful and wealthy Julia Franklin, but
his guilt over Charlotte prevents his proposing marriage. Montraville's false friend, Belcour, who would like to have Charlotte as his
own mistress, treacherously convinces Montraville that Charlotte is
unfaithful and persuades Charlotte that Montraville has left her for
another woman. Pregnant and abandoned, Charlotte is turned out of
her lodging and struggles through a snowstorm to seek assistance
from her former friend and French teacher, LaRue. But LaRue has
been installed comfortably in a luxurious home and enjoys a social position that she refuses to jeopardize by acknowledging Charlotte. Finally taken in by some poor servants, Charlotte gives birth to a
daughter and becomes insane. Her father arrives from England just in
time to forgive her before she dies, and he brings home to his heart-
broken wife not their lost daughter but their orphaned grandchild,
Lucy. The novel ends with Belcour's death in a duel, LaRue dying
penniless and alone, and Montraville "to the end of his life subject to
fits of melancholy."

Rowson subtitled this novel "A Tale of Truth" and attested in the
preface that the story had been told to her by a woman acquainted
with Charlotte and that she as author had merely "thrown over the
whole a slight veil of fiction, substituting names and places according
to her fancy." In none of her previous works had Rowson insisted
upon the truth of her fiction, leaving that practice to those novelists
who feared the moral censure fiction often received. Rowson had never
worried about moral censure of her books, for she felt confident of
their didactic value and certain they could never lead a young reader
to harm. Now that she did insist upon the authenticity of a novel,
she was believed, and by the early years of the nineteenth century
detective-fans of *Charlotte* concluded that the heroine was in fact Char-

lotte Stanley, daughter of the eleventh earl of Derby, and Montraville was in real life John Montresor, Rowson's cousin.

Evidence supports the conclusion that Montraville was based upon the life of Montresor. Lt. John Montresor was the son of Susanna Rowson's father's sister, Mary Haswell, who married John Gabriel Montresor, an army engineer. Lt. John Montresor was therefore Rowson's cousin, though twenty-seven years older than she. Like his father, John Montresor also became an army engineer and worked extensively along the east coast of North America, serving as the principal engineer in Boston and New York when the British occupied those cities during the Revolution. When Susanna was still a baby, her cousin had married Frances Tucker of Bermuda, who bore him ten children. In the same year that the Haswells moved back to England, 1778, John Montresor and his family also returned to England to settle.[28] It is not impossible that Rowson modeled her novel after a family story about this glamorous older cousin, whose many adventures in the American colonies and whose later wealth provided the Haswells with sources of comment and speculation. The same Montresor seems to have served as model for the character Montraville in *Charlotte's Daughter*.

Less evidence exists for the popularly held view that the source for the character of Charlotte Temple was Charlotte Stanley, daughter of the eleventh earl of Derby. Charlotte Stanley eloped in 1743 with John Burgoyne (1722–1792), whereupon her father gave her only a small amount of money and declared he would never see her again. Years later the couple reconciled with the earl, who ultimately left his daughter £25,000. Rowson may have been familiar with Burgoyne, for he wrote for the London stage and had a lengthy affair with a popular singer.[29] She never denied the validity of the Montresor-Stanley story, being fully conscious of its publicity value.

Charlotte is the shortest of Rowson's novels. It is narrated in the third person, with an occasional first-person comment inserted by the author. The book opens with the main story line, then switches in chapter two to the history of Charlotte Temple's father and in chapter three to the history of Charlotte's grandfather; chapter ten introduces another brief interruption, the history of Montraville's family. But other than these brief subplots the main story proceeds rapidly and smoothly. One early twentieth-century critic, Lillie Deming Loshe, correctly commented that "there are many such tales, treated merely as episodes in Mrs. Rowson's other novels, which, if worked out separately with the same brevity and workmanlike construction, might have won the same reputation."[30] The simplicity and conciseness of *Charlotte* distinguish it from the two other popular Richardsonian novels by American authors during this period, *The Power of Sympathy* (1789) by William Hill Brown and *The Coquette* (1797) by Hannah Webster Foster. Both these works employ the epistolary format, with digressions and subplots weaving long and complex story lines. In *Charlotte* Rowson unfolds her plot more rapidly than in any other of her novels, but significant scenes receive dramatic focus. Perhaps recalling her theatrical experience, Rowson details important scenes involving main characters and often condenses dialogue and combines it with narration, as in this abduction scene:

"Now, said Montraville, taking Charlotte in his arms, "you are mine forever."

"No," said she, withdrawing from his embrace. "I am come to take an everlasting farewel."

It would be useless to repeat the conversation that here ensued; suffice it to say, that Montraville used every argument that had formerly been successful, Charlotte's resolution began to waver, and he drew her almost imperceptibly towards the chaise.

"I cannot go," said she: "cease, dear Montraville, to persuade. I must not: religion, duty, forbid."

"Cruel Charlotte," said he, "if you disappoint my ardent hopes, by all that is sacred, this hand shall put a period to my existence. I cannot—will not live without you."

"Alas! my torn heart!" said Charlotte, "how shall I act?"

"Let me direct you," said Montraville, lifting her into the chaise.

"Oh! my dear forsaken parents!" cried Charlotte.

The chaise drove off. She shrieked, and fainted into the arms of her betrayer.[31]

This novel differs from Rowson's others in its simplicity and conciseness, but it resembles her other works in its editorial and didactic comments. At times Rowson addressed her reader personally as she had done occasionally in previous novels:

O my dear girls, for to such only am I writing, listen not to the voice of love unless sanctioned by paternal approbation; be assured it is now past the days of romance. (60)

A few pages later, after digressing from the story with a moral lecture, Rowson justified her methods to her reader:

I confess I have rambled strangely from my story; but what of that? if I have been so lucky as to find the road to happiness, why should I be such a niggard as to omit so good an opportunity to pointing out the way to others. (67)

When she came to a particularly poignant scene, the author made sure her readers grasped its significance. "My dear young readers, I would have you read this scene with attention" (90). And Rowson identified with her young readers when she satirized her own sentimental style:

'Bless my heart,' cries my young, volatile reader, 'I shall never have patience to get through these volumes, there are so many ahs! and ohs! so much fainting, tears, and distress, I am sick to death of the subject.' (139)

These direct addresses reveal the author's awareness of the reader, and this personal, conversational approach again contrasts sharply with the epistolary form of contemporary American novels such as *The Power of Sympathy* and *The Coquette*.

Charlotte differs from the typical Rowson heroine by succumbing to a seducer and suffering for her mistake. Rowson's first fictional heroine, Victoria, is the only other of all her many women characters who commits a similar crime, and she too suffers the conventional fate of childbirth and death. Charlotte submits to Montraville because she is young and inexperienced and because she is encouraged by a woman she trusts. Charlotte's acquaintances have, before boarding school, included only family and childhood friends, so she is unprepared for the selfish wiles of Madame LaRue. She has no defense against this worldly and clever woman who knows exactly how to persuade Charlotte to act according to her wishes. Charlotte has been taught the difference between good and bad by her doting parents, but, perhaps because she has so entirely relied upon them, she is indecisive and is easily convinced that both LaRue and Montraville care for her with the same devotion she has always known from her parents. Several times she decides against seeing Montraville only to have LaRue change her mind, for LaRue knows that Charlotte must inevitably fall prey to lies and flattery from a handsome young man in uniform.

Despite Charlotte's inexperience, Rowson held her responsible for her actions. As Charlotte consents to meet Montraville at LaRue's urging, Charlotte determines "never to repeat the indiscretion." "But alas!" comments the narrator, "poor Charlotte, she knew not the deceitfulness of her own heart, or she would have avoided the trial of her stability" (71). She falls victim to the schemes of LaRue and Montraville and to "her too great sensibility." Rowson went so far as to say "no woman can be run away with contrary to her own inclination" (609).

LaRue is Rowson's most fully developed villain. To explain her persistent villainy Rowson wrote:

When once a woman has stifled the sense of shame in her own bosom, when once she has lost sight of her basis on which reputation, honour, everything that should be dear to the female heart, rests, she grows hardened in guilt, and will spare no pains to bring down innocence and beauty to the shocking level with herself. (64)

Thus Rowson clearly indicated her belief that vice has no respect for gender. LaRue is simply evil. She destroys the happiness of Charlotte, Montraville, and Colonel Crayton. She manipulates Montraville as readily as she exploits Charlotte, for both offer her a means of escaping her detested teaching position and of rejoining the world, where she can achieve the wealth and social position she seeks. She uses and discards Belcour and Colonel Crayton, and she so cruelly turns out into the street the pregnant Charlotte that even her lover is shocked. For all her wickedness LaRue is fittingly punished with poverty and sickness.

Rowson believed in retribution. Montraville, the actual seducer, suffers a lesser punishment than LaRue because he is not so guilty. (He is permitted to live and to marry the woman he loves. LaRue must die.) Montraville is, in fact, quite likable, "generous in his disposition, liberal in his opinions, and good natured almost to a fault." He pursues Charlotte with the impetuosity of youth. "He staid not to reflect on the consequences which might follow the attainment of his wishes" (70). No Lovelace, Montraville loves Charlotte but lacks the maturity to reflect on the strength of his love or the consequences of their "elopement." A number of coincidences contribute to the acts for which Montraville must take blame: Belcour would never have tricked Montraville into believing Charlotte unfaithful had he not seen Montraville approach the house while Charlotte lay sleeping; Charlotte would not have contracted an illness from exposure if Mrs. Beauchamp had been there to take her in; and so on. Rowson thus created a seducer who himself is victimized, by a woman, by his friend, and by circumstance. Such a complex view of male villainy did not typify seduction novels and contributed to *Charlotte*'s air of credibility.

Belcour is the other real villain in this plot, and he, like LaRue, has no redeeming virtues. Though he never originates deceit, he exploits situations to his advantage. When he sees Montraville approach the house, he suddenly decides to lie down next to the sleeping Charlotte, placing the girl in such a compromising position that Montraville will be convinced of her unfaithfulness. He never succeeds in taking Charlotte as his own mistress, but he suffers death at Montraville's hands as his appropriately melodramatic end.

Following the conventional doctrine, Rowson taught in *Charlotte* that young women need parental guidance in a world where men will try to seduce them. Beyond this usual seduction motif, she also taught that unsophisticated schoolgirls need guidance against other challenges: an unscrupulous school teacher who uses the naïveté of her students to better her position; a landlady who will exercise no pity when the rent is due; life in an unfamiliar environment without women friends for guidance.

Rowson's emphasis on the virtues of the middle class contributed to the book's popularity among later American readers. Although Mr. Temple is the youngest son of an earl and heir to only £500 a year, he forgoes marriage to an heiress in order to marry the woman he loves. Unlike the romantic plot of the hypothetical novel described in *The Inquisitor*, this marriage for love brings not poverty, but "Plenty," for neither Temple nor his wife has extravagant habits, and they live comfortably in a "cottage," caring for their cows and poultry. They have enough money to support Temple's father-in-law and to send their daughter to boarding school. Mrs. Beauchamp is another example of middle-class rectitude. Although she is the daughter of the wealthy Colonel Crayton, she finds her domestic happiness in a small house in the country. These are the only two happy marriages in the story, and the American audience appreciated this idealization of the "middle sphere" of life.

At the same time, Rowson may be suggesting in this presentation of Temple's life that Temple is overly romantic. He disobeys his father to marry the woman he loves and thus becomes the only "good" character in all Rowson's fiction to defy parents without immediate reprisal. Though he and his wife and father-in-law and daughter live contentedly for many years, ultimately he suffers the loss of his daughter and the end of his happiness. Rowson implies that Temple suffers from sensibilities greater than his reason. Certainly he overprotects his daughter and educates her inadequately for the realities of life. The lesson for parents here is that to merit filial piety from their offspring, they must first provide their children with a proper preparation for life.

Rowson also repeated in *Charlotte* her disapproval of class snobbery. This time she used strong language to state her antipathy toward marriage for wealth or rank. She made her young Mr. Temple refuse to marry unless he loved, because he had seen the consequences of marriage for the wrong reasons:

He saw his eldest brother made completely wretched by marrying a disagreeable woman, whose fortune helped to prop the sinking dignity of the house, and he beheld his sisters legally prostituted to old, decrepit men, whose titles gave them consequence in the eyes of the world, and whose affluence rendered them splendidly miserable. (40)

Rowson did not mince words in describing her beliefs. Such views held just enough romanticism to appeal to the American middle classes, but not so much that Rowson need fear censure for corrupting youth.

Charlotte met with only a slightly more favorable critical response in England than her other novels had received. The *Critical Review* found the book "a tale of real distress" and praised the plot and descriptions. The reviewer sympathized with Charlotte, who "scarcely perhaps deserved so severe a punishment." Still unsure of the truth of the novel, the reviewer concluded, "If it is a fiction, poetic justice is not, we think, properly distributed."[32] This review is reprinted, as advertisement, in both the first and second American editions published in Philadelphia in 1794.

Rebecca; or, the Fille de Chambre

The last novel Rowson published in England was *Rebecca; or, the Fille de Chambre* (1792), a novel which, like *Charlotte*, was later to become popular in the United States. In the preface to *Rebecca* Rowson promised to write an unromantic book with no "wonderful discoveries of titles, rank, and wealth being unexpectedly heaped upon [the heroine]."[33] This intention was consistent with her earlier disapproval of books that glorified wealth and title or that led readers to believe that love conquers all. Rowson herself was a sensible woman, and she frowned upon excessive romanticism in others. She also introduced in the preface the main theme of the novel. In a dialogue between herself and "Mr. Puffendorf," who likes to read only about aristocrats, Rowson protests that "a woman may be an interesting character tho' placed in the humblest walks of life," and this idea of character and virtue rising above rank becomes the central theme of the novel.[34]

The story revolves around Rebecca Littleton, the daughter of a retired army lieutenant. Rebecca's humble fortunes rise when she is taken into the home of Lady Mary Worthy but fall again when both her father and her patron die within weeks of each other. The heroine is soon on her own in the world and encounters a number of adventures including a trip to America before she finally settles down.

The book is notable for its autobiographical passages.[35] The character of Rebecca resembles Rowson herself. Rebecca at sixteen, with neither rank nor fortune, is naive and unprepared for the world, similar to Susanna Haswell upon her arrival in London during the Revolutionary War:

She harbored no thought which fear or shame prevented her revealing, for this reason, her actions and sentiments were often open to the malevolent mis-constructions of those who, having art enough to conceal the real impulse of their natures, assume the assemblance of . . . virtues. (6)

She values hard work and will do anything respectable to support herself. "I do not wish to eat the bread of idleness," she says. In the 1814 preface Rowson singled out several particular scenes drawn directly from her own life, such as the scene at Lady Ossiter's. Lady Ossiter, Rebecca's employer, is vain and cruel; she deprives Rebecca of the inheritance Lady Mary Worthy intended for her; and she feels jealous of Rebecca's youthful appearance and good nature. She makes of Rebecca a veritable servant, and her spoiled and uncontrollable children tax Rebecca's considerable patience. Though Rebecca tries her best to please Lady Ossiter, she is horrified when Lady Ossiter tries to enlist her aid in concealing love affairs from her husband. Lord Ossiter, himself unfaithful, tries to seduce Rebecca and thereby drives her from the house.[36]

The American episode is also autobiographical, Rowson attested, beginning with the vividly detailed sea voyage and ice storm that nearly sinks Rebecca's ship within sight of Boston. Rowson convincingly related Rebecca's astonishment when she first views a New England winter scene: "A new world now opened on Rebecca . . . every object was bound in the frigid chains of winter. The harbour, which she could see from the house on the island, was one continued sheet of ice" (117). Later Rowson described the village on Nantasket peninsula where the Haswells lived, an idyllic New England village whose tranquillity is disturbed by the onset of the Revolution. Rowson omitted details of her childhood but described vividly her experiences in the war. Her account of incidents that she herself witnessed or participated in, such as the burning of the Boston lighthouse and the death of the soldier left in the Haswell (Abthorpe) house, gives the war a chilling immediacy and sharpness. With brutal realism she recalled one soldier saying of his wounded companion, "D——n him . . . he is in our way; if he don't die quickly we will kill him" (122). When the soldier dies of his wounds, Rebecca and the Abthorpe family bury him quickly because of the heat. This American adventure section of *Rebecca* is one of the author's best in its realistic presentation of detail, its lively dialogue, and its sympathetic character delineation. It holds significance in the history of American fiction as an early account of war experiences.

Rowson did not acknowledge the autobiographical aspects of *Rebecca* in the 1792 edition perhaps because at that time she had no reason to defend her national affiliations; no one had yet questioned her political loyalty. But by 1814 she had become sensitive to criticism of her status in America as a British woman, as she complained in a letter to a cousin in Vermont.[37] Rowson's later assertion that she felt divided between love of her mother country and love for her adopted country is borne out in her description of the war. She sympathized with both sides, and her father refused to espouse either until late in the war when the Americans forced him to evacuate.

Although *Rebecca* is less didactic than *Mary* or *Mentoria*, the themes in this novel repeat those Rowson used in previous fiction. As usual, she stressed filial piety, although in *Rebecca* filial obedience expands, not to include obedience to God, as in *Mentoria*, but to include respect for all those older and wiser. Rebecca mourns the death of her patron as she would have mourned for her own mother, for example, and she later experiences the same filial gratitude toward an uncle that she felt for her father when he lived. Second, acceptance of one's station is related to Rowson's emphasis on the middle class. Rebecca knows she should not marry the nobly born Sir George Worthy, but she also refuses to become one of the household servants. She marries Sir George only when his common birth is uncovered and heartily agrees when he exclaims, "abundance of riches cannot secure happiness!" The "middle sphere," however, requires more than love for sustenance, so George inherits an estate, and Rebecca brings £2000 to the marriage. Third, as a woman from the "humble walk of life," Rebecca illustrates Rowson's faith in virtue unconnected to rank. This idea is introduced in the prefatory dialogue with Mr. Puffendorf and is repeated in the characterization of the Ossiters. Both Lord and Lady Ossiter consider themselves socially superior to Rebecca, but their adultery and selfishness prove them moral inferiors. This democracy of good and evil appealed especially to American readers, and *Rebecca* enjoyed a success in the United States second only to *Charlotte* among Rowson's other works.

These themes suggest Rowson's continuing interest in her audience of young women and their education. Rebecca is in every way a heroine Rowson would happily have seen her readers emulate. In part Rebecca's behavior reflects her education. After a thorough grounding in the "tenets of the protestant religion," with attendant instruction in behavior and decorum proper to middle-class English ladies, Rebecca is permitted to receive instruction in drawing and music. But she knows enough to regard these arts as "pastime," not part of her serious education. This training together with her character and good sense see Rebecca through a formidable series of adventures.

In addition to this novel's autobiographical interest and thematic consistency, *Rebecca* has stylistic qualities to recommend it. As in other successful Rowson novels, Rebecca's adventures unfold rapidly and clearly, despite the quantity of episodes. Further, dialogue, character sketches, and drawing-room comedy scenes are presented with a humorous touch sometimes lacking in her other novels. In an extended dialogue early in the novel, for example, Lord Ossiter's sarcasm is lost on Lady Ossiter, so that the reader feels amused at the cruel lady's expense. Abigail Penure, whose characteristics are suggested by her name, is presented with satiric wit and provides another humorous moment. And more than once Rowson drew upon her theatrical background for presentation of a scene, once even recalling a particular play for the reader. "Rebecca was desired to walk into a parlor, where, in his nightgown and slippers, sat a personage, the exact counterpart of Lord Ogleby, in the Clandestine Marriage" (209).

Nevertheless, *Rebecca* does not succeed without impediment. When Rowson seems in command of her material, the novel amuses and moves along smoothly, but when she relies upon the devices of the formulaic fiction of her day, the book flags. Rowson is not above the old tricks of deus ex machina when she needs a hasty solution. When Rebecca is evicted from her position because she has unconsciously attracted her employer, she manages to leave the country in a quick two paragraphs. Later, when the author wants her heroine to marry George Worthy without breaking her promise to Lady Mary Worthy never to marry her son, Rowson has only to rely upon a trick found in much cheap popular fiction. The deathbed confession of an ancient nurse suddenly proves that Sir George is in fact not Sir George, and a birthmark identifies him as a commoner, switched in the cradle.

To publish this novel Rowson returned to William Lane, the publisher of her last two novels. Lane published only one edition of *Rebecca*, in 1792, and as yet no copies of this first edition have been located. The novel was pirated the following year by the same Dublin booksellers who printed an edition of *Mentoria*. No critical reviews have been located.

Thus between 1786 and 1792 Susanna Rowson published six novels, firmly establishing herself as a writer of fiction for women. She had moved from the complex plot of *Victoria* to the effective simplicity of *Charlotte*. She had increased her confidence so that she could move from an obscure publisher to the aggressively successful William Lane. Through all her writings she had remained faithful to her own beliefs and written nothing she could regret. She believed wholeheartedly in the standards of behavior she advocated in all her novels, and in a few years she was to find an even more effective means of instruction.

Chapter Three
Literature of the Stage

A *Trip to Parnassus*

Rowson's first publication suggests her early involvement with the theater. In 1788 she published *A Trip to Parnassus; or, the Judgment of Apollo on Dramatic Authors and Performers*, a thirty-page, lighthearted work inscribed to Thomas Harris, manager of the theater at Covent Garden.[1] The poem describes in couplets of anapestic quatrameter the approach to Apollo's throne of some thirty-four actors and writers. With merciless abruptness Apollo either welcomes them with bay leaves and laurels or casts them aside as undeserving of praise.

The poem reflects an intimate acquaintance with the performers and writers of Covent Garden, one of London's three patent theaters, and it reflects Rowson's considerable interest in theater art. Almost all of the actors who come before Apollo for judgment were part of the Covent Garden company, and the writers were those whose works constituted part of the company repertoire. Except Sheridan, few of the dramatists are recognizable today, for with the notable exception of Sheridan and Goldsmith, late eighteenth-century theater engaged the attention of only second- or third-rate writers. Few distinguished plays were written during Rowson's theatrical career. Most of the best acting appeared in the comedy and other light genres, and those are the forms that attracted Rowson. She liked especially the sentimental comedies of Elizabeth Inchbald, John O'Keefe, and the George Colmans, senior and junior.

The dramatists appear first in *Parnassus*. The first playwright she brought for Apollonian judgment was Edward Topham, a dramatist known for his sartorial taste. But Rowson disliked vanity, and so she dismissed him quickly:

> The first that advanc'd, without order or rule,
> Was that Tip-Top* of taste, whose first borne was a Fool.
> Apollo, displeas'd, push'd the upstart away.
>
> (3)

"The Fool" was Topham's second, not first, play, a farce in two acts performed at Covent Garden and printed in 1786.[2]

As corollary to her disapproval of vanity, Rowson held morality up as a standard for the writing of drama, a position shared by most eighteenth-century playwrights, who stressed the rewards of virtue. Thus she praised George Colman, the second dramatist introduced to Apollo, for his "honour and virtue":

> ". . . a man in [Apollo's] service grown grey,
> Who, pourtraying the heart of a Freeport, has shown
> The honour and virtue which glow in his own:
> The Deity smiled, and the Muses drew near
> To welcome a brother they ever held dear.
>
> (3)

Colman at age fifty-six continued to act as proprietor of Covent Garden despite the effects of a paralytic stroke suffered three years earlier. A writer and adapter of some thirty dramatic pieces, he had spent his inheritance on the purchase of Covent Garden Theatre in 1767.[3]

Rowson repeated her belief in drama as purveyor of virtue in a novel she published the following year, *Mary; or, the Test of Honour*. The title character, an avid theatergoer, calls for moral drama:

Why are there such scenes represented on the stage as we should blush to see practiced in private life? Why cannot all their comedies be written in the same chaste style which some are? It appears to me highly improper to represent before an audience, the greatest part of which are composed of the youthful of both sexes, scenes of immoral tendency, which may not only be a means of leading them into numerous errors, but may corrupt and vitiate their minds in such a manner as to be an irreparable injury to the rising generation (43).

Rowson held to her standards of moral taste, regardless of popular opinion. Hannah Cowley, for example, had written many plays that met with audience acclaim at both Drury Lane and Covent Garden, but Rowson did not approve of her works and did not fail to say so:

> Next Cowley approach'd, but Apollo looked down,
> While his features divine were deform'd by a frown;
> 'Hold, woman (he cried) approach not too near,
> 'I dictate no line that can wound the chaste ear;

'When your sex take the pen, it is shocking to find,
'From their writing loose thoughts have a place in their mind.'

(4)

A similar objection to Cowley was expressed in the *Gentleman's Maga-zine*.[4]

As for acting, Rowson's standard was naturalness, an ideal she sought in her own stage performances as well as in her literary pro-ductions. The semblance of natural behavior on stage was in the eigh-teenth century by no means a given, especially in performance of tragedy. The "roaring styles" of tragic representation had been re-placed in the eighteenth century by an "indolently-dignified, monoto-nous declamation" which failed to distinguish one tragic character from another except by costume. Rowson would have agreed with this contemporary description of James Quin, who epitomized this style of acting:

With very little variation of cadency, and in a deep, full tone, accompanied by a sawing kind of action, which had more of the senate than of the stage in it, he rolled out his heroics with an air of dignified indifference that seemed to disdain the plaudits that were bestowed upon him. Unable to ex-press emotions, whether violent or tender, he was forced or languid in action and ponderous and sluggish in movement.[5]

Rowson and others who shared her preference for natural acting may have been influenced by David Garrick, who had sought to change this declamatory style of tragic performance. Garrick had endeavored to make tragic characters more real by introducing variety in their representation. He had tried to replace the conventional rhetorical techniques with individuality in characters that even the dullest audi-ence could recognize as distinctive. As stage manager of Drury Lane for thirty years, he had tried to teach others his techniques, but his principles were slow to spread. Though Rowson had never seen Gar-rick, who had retired two years before her return to England, she ad-hered to at least some of his principles. "Make Nature your copy," she advised.

Another famous actor who had introduced realism into his charac-ters was Charles Macklin. Rowson so enthusiastically approved of his techniques that she gave him an especially long section in her poem. "To dame Nature you've paid due regard," Rowson's Apollo said, "And trod in the steps of my favourite bard." Apollo's "favourite

bard" was of course Shakespeare, for Macklin had made his career
with his portrayal of Shylock. Instead of playing the Jew as a comic
buffoon, which had long been the tradition, Macklin made him an
obstinate, passionate man—much like Macklin himself. This new interpretation had been enthusiastically received ever since Macklin had
first played the role at Drury Lane in 1741. Macklin was still performing his Shylock even as he approached the age of eighty, and
Rowson had seen and delighted in his creation:

> Could Shakespeare himself from the silent tomb rise,
> He'd view your performance with joyful surprise;
> And charm'd with your excellence, freely wou'd own,
> That Macklin in Shylock can ne'er be out-done.
>
> (10)

Perhaps her insistence upon a natural acting style influenced her
preference for comic over tragic drama, for comic art, never having
lapsed into stiff and colorless declamation, produced better acting.
Rowson's preference for comedy may account for her association with
Covent Garden, where more comedies than serious plays were being
produced.

But Rowson was not so naive as to believe an actor could act "naturally" without concerted effort. "There is genius and judgment in acting required." She advised one aspiring young actress to perform with
genuine feeling:

> . . . beauty alone will not do on the stage.
> You must have animation, must feel what you speak.
> Call a tear to your eye, or a blush to your cheek.
> It is wrong, on the stage, when performing a part,
> Like a school girl, to con o'er your lesson by heart.
> The merely repeating a speech will not do;
> You must feel it yourself, and make others feel too.
> A public performer must study to please,
> And for public applause, must give up their own ease.
> A task that's more difficult scarce can be known
> Than an actress to please the caprice of the town.
>
> (18)

Rowson may have learned the necessity of feeling a part intently from
Sarah Siddons, who, it was said, never spoke a line on stage that she

did not feel. Rowson found much to admire in the great Siddons, who combined beauty, talent, hard work, and an emotional commitment to her profession with a virtuous personal life.[6] As such personal role models seemed important to the young and ambitious Rowson, she later searched through history to find models for other young women.

In addition to presenting Rowson's theories of dramatic art, *A Trip to Parnassus* expressed her view of one contemporary issue, the opening of the Royalty Theatre. In this controversy Rowson sided conservatively with the established theaters and thus showed herself as the rather proper, conservative woman she would remain all her life. The Royalty Theatre had been built in 1785 in Wellclose Square by John Palmer (1742–98), an actor whose career seemed dogged by misfortune.[7] Against the advice of theatrical friends, he opened on June 20, 1787. The managers of the three patent theaters so successfully fought his efforts to obtain the necessary licenses that the Royalty closed after the first performance. A pamphlet war ensued. On July 3 Palmer reopened for the performance of "pantomime and irregular pieces," anything not defined as a "play." Despite her interest in pantomime and light entertainment for the masses, Rowson frowned upon this arrangement, which attracted crowds and thereby reduced audiences at the large patent theaters. Others found nothing wrong with it, however, and several actors, among them one Mary Wells, left Covent Garden for a few weeks to take advantage of Palmer's extravagant salaries. To applauding Royalty audiences Mary Wells mimicked great actresses such as Siddons, but for her troubles she earned Rowson's condemnation. "She had never much claim to my favour," said Apollo.

> And her folly has made me abjure her for ever.
> Then angry commanded her hence to be hurl'd,
> And declar'd she had praises enough in the World.[8]
>
> (13)

Rowson described John Palmer himself as a "poor Pantomimical hero," whose youthful fame would wither with age (17). She was, unfortunately for Palmer, correct.

Despite the seriousness of much of *A Trip to Parnassus*, Rowson's tone throughout the poem was light. In the end she brought forward her narrator to direct the last laugh at herself. (Recall that in *The In-*

quisitor she used the narrator as a main character throughout the book.) From the throng of dramatists and performers pressing to appear before Apollo, Rowson herself steps up to the god. That she who had as yet neither produced a play nor appeared on a London stage should dare to join the company of accomplished playwrights and actors suggests her courage and willingness to assert herself. But she knew her limits, felt a decorous modesty, and would go only so far. Rowson's Apollo rejects her narrator, though she is spared the actual sentence:

> He seem'd much offended, and gave me a look,
> To see it, the Muses themselves must have shook.
> Thick clouds gather'd round him, the hollow winds howl'd,
> The blue lightnings flash'd, and the hoarse thunder roll'd'
> I fell prostrate before him, and fain wou'd have spoke,
> But my fears were so great, that I trembling awoke.
>
> (26)

And thus the poem ends.

A Trip to Parnassus shows Rowson's early interest in and skill with rhyme. The poem uses full, near, and internal rhymes, and the lines contain simple sound patterns of assonance, consonance, and alliteration. But she attempted nothing more complicated, as her more natural mode was prose, not poetry, and though she published *Poems on Various Subjects*[9] in London the same year, she did not again attempt poetry for many years.

Perhaps because it was her first publication, Rowson published *A Trip to Parnassus* anonymously. She dedicated the book to Thomas Harris, manager of the Covent Garden theater, whose company provided the subject matter. She sold the manuscript to John Abraham, a relatively small publisher in St. Swithin's Lane, Lombard Street, London, who printed the book as a quarto and sold it for two shillings.

A Trip to Parnassus received a mildly favorable review in the *Monthly Review*:

The plan of the "Session of the Poets," by Sir John Suckling, hath been adopted by many of the sons of Apollo, with various success, from Rochester and Mulgrave, down to the author of the "Children of Thespis," and the fair writer of this *poetical* dream: who is not the least successful of Suckling's imitators; and is a much better versifier than was Sir John—though Congreve styled him *natural* and easy. —In appreciating the respective merits of our present race of dramatic authors, and actors, she is careful to throw out no reflection on private characters; but, as public performers, whether in the closet or *on the boards*, she considers them as proper objects of critical investigation. . . .[10]

But the *Critical Review* of the same month judged her first effort more harshly. Calling her a fly without a sting, the reviewer disagreed with her evaluations of dramatists and actors but admitted that she was more inclined to praise than blame and would not "sacrifice each well-meaning candidate for fame, to raise a pile to some favourite idol of fashion or prejudice." Of her verse, the reviewer said, it had neither "gross defects" nor "striking beauties."[11]

American Publications

Slaves in Algiers.   As a member of Thomas Wignell's Philadelphia acting company, Rowson contributed her several skills. In addition to acting she wrote lyrics and plays. Her first American play, *Slaves in Algiers*, was hastily conceived and executed, taking no more than two months from conception to first performance. Thanks to one irate critic, however, the play received publicity for months.

Slaves in Algiers capitalized on current interest in attacks on American ships by Barbary pirates. Rowson had known in England of the piracy of the Barbary states, Algiers, Morocco, Tripoli, and Tunis. From her father she had long ago learned that the worst among them were the Algerians, and that their practice of capturing goods, ships, and men had gone on since English ships had first sailed the seas. Italian, Spanish, and German ships also suffered these attacks, not only in the Mediterranean but far into the Atlantic. By paying ransom, these nations had encouraged the piracy, and now the Barbary governments sought to extract the same blackmail from the United States. In America Rowson learned of the new nation's concern with the problem, for America had been losing ships and captives to Algerian pirates in the Mediterranean for about ten years. When the United States refused to pay tribute to the Dey of Algiers, American ships, like the English and Europeans before them, suffered degrading abuse. By the time Rowson arrived in Philadelphia, well over a hundred American sailors were enslaved in Algiers and more were being brought in weekly.

Rowson's play was not the only literary work to capitalize on the resentment Americans were feeling.[12] In 1787 Royall Tyler published *The Algerine Captive*, and in 1794 the bookseller Mathew Carey wrote *A Short Account of Algiers*. Rowson may have read Carey's forty-six page account, which contained a general description of Algeria, a chapter on customs and religion, another on the origin of the present government, and a discussion entitled "The State of America as to Algiers." Carey mentioned no names of particular places in Algiers, but he did refer to the many gardens and to the use of rows of fig trees for walls. Rowson set her scenes in palace gardens and hid her characters behind fig trees, but she too seemed only slightly acquainted or little concerned with specific facts about the nation. She did know that olives and figs grew there and that Jews lived among the Moors without discrimination. Rowson's interest, however, lay not in Algeria itself but in the subject of tyranny in general and of tyranny of men over women in particular. She used this popular topic to make her first feminist statement on stage.

The plot involves a beautiful young woman, Olivia, who has been captured by Algerian pirates and sold to Muley Moloc, the Dey of Algiers. The character of Olivia derived from the character of Semira the Greek in Rowson's earlier novel, *Mary; or, the Test of Honour*, and it seems significant that Rowson transformed her into an American for her American audience. Olivia's father, Constant, and her fiancé, Henry, have separately had themselves captured in attempts to free Olivia. To this story is added the subplot of Fetnah, the outspoken and courageous daughter of the Jew, Ben Hassan. Fetnah has been taught to love liberty and independence by Rebecca, an American woman prisoner to Ben Hassan. Fetnah falls in love with another Christian slave, Frederic, and longs to escape to democratic America with her Christian lover. All of these prisoners contrive an escape under the plan of Zoriana, the daughter of the Dey and a secret convert to Christianity. When Olivia learns that Zoriana has fallen in love with her own fiancé Henry, Olivia decides not to try to escape with the others but to stay behind and sacrifice herself to the Dey's wrath. The escape fails, so Olivia, secretly planning suicide, offers herself in marriage to the Dey if he will permit her father and fiancé to go free. Suddenly a slave revolt leaves Muley Moloc helplessly surrounded, so he agrees to free all Algerian captives and provide for their passage home. Olivia is united with Henry, and in a standard recognition scene Rebecca finds her long-lost husband and daughter—none other than Constant and Olivia.

As this plot summary shows, the play was contrived, the characters stereotyped, and the language stilted, and yet it enjoyed a surprising popularity. It became a part of the repertoire of the Philadelphia company and was performed in Baltimore as well as in Philadelphia. Unlike most plays written during this period, *Slaves* was sufficiently well received to merit publication, and Rowson had it printed the same year it was first produced.[13]

How can the play's popularity be accounted for? Rowson's name alone could not have caused the play to succeed, even though she had a slight reputation as actress at the New Theater, and she had begun to create a reading public through republication of her earlier novels. A more likely factor would have been the topic of the play and its American chauvinism. Although Rowson created this play as a revision of a brief subplot from her earlier novel *Mary; or, The Test of Honour*, she altered it to appeal to an American audience. She changed the heroine from Semira, a captive Greek, to Olivia, a young American woman, and she made all the main characters American—patriotic Americans at that. Whereas in *A Test of Honour* England served as Rowson's symbol of liberty and democracy, in *Slaves* she transferred that symbol to America. She dedicated the printed version to "the citizens of the United-States of North-America." An additional appeal, at least for some audiences, was that the American chauvinism in the play served the larger purpose of celebrating the concept of freedom for all people. The plot involving prisoners for ransom permitted Rowson to contrast an oppressive with a free society:

> Who barters countrymen, honour, faith, to save
> His life, tho' free in person, is a slave.
> While he, enchan'd, imprison'd tho he be,
> Who lifts his arm for liberty, is free.[14]

Rowson's slave characters suffer the same longings for freedom as an imprisoned American feels. The author's comments about liberty would have been well received by democrats in the pit, at a time when feelings about the French Revolution still ran high.

Significantly, this political rhetoric did not occur in Rowson's novels and stories, nor was it found in novels by other authors before

1800, though it was found frequently in poetry and drama. The reading public in the United States at that time, thought to consist largely of young, unmarried women, was considerably smaller than the numbers who regularly attended the theater. That theater audience was comparatively unrestrained. They interrupted a musical number with demands to hear "Yankee Doodle," and threw gin bottles and orange peels if they did not get it. They loved to hear repeated praise for American patriotism and virtue.[15] Rowson had worked in the Chestnut Street Theater for only one year when she wrote *Slaves in Algiers*, but she was obviously sensitive to the nationalistic rhetoric and the demands of her theater audience.

Rowson carried her rhetoric about America and liberty a step further. If all men love and need freedom, then the same is true for women, and Rowson joined the love of political liberty with the love of sexual liberty. She put into the character of Fetnah her most outspoken comments on the position of women. Fetnah has been taught by another English woman captive and has herself come to believe in women's inequality:

Woman was never formed to be the abject slave of man. Nature made us equal with them, and gave us the power to render ourselves superior. (1.1.9)
. . . A woman can face danger with as much spirit, and as little fear as the bravest man amongst you. (3.1.47)

Fetnah objects particularly to her own sexual enslavement to a man she does not love, for, she claims, women as well as men love freedom:

> Woman when by nature drest
> In charms devoid of art
> Can warm the stoic's icy breast,
> Can triumph o'er each heart.
> Can bid the soul to virtue rise,
> To glory prompt the brave,
> But sinks oppress'd and drooping dies,
> When once she's made a slave.
>   (1.1.10)

When asked if she does not love her master, Fetnah's reply indicates Rowson's rejection of sexual dominance or forced "love":

No—he is old and ugly,—then he wears such tremendous whiskers, and when he makes love, he looks so grave and stately, that I declare, if it was not for his huge scymitar, I shou'd burst out a laughing in his face. (1.1.6)

Fetnah's enforced subservience makes the sexual relationship, emphasized with phallic symbolism, repugnant to her. She plainly states her objection to slavery:

I think I see him now . . . a long pipe in his mouth. Oh! how charmingly the tobacco must perfume his whiskers—here, Mustapha, says he, 'Go bid the slave Selima come to me'—well it does not signify,—I wonder how any woman of spirit can gulp it down. (2.2.39)

Rowson did not here reject male sexuality but tyranny based on sex, the use of women as sexual commodities. Fetnah longs for both physical freedom from her position as slave and the freedom of a genuine sexual love. She wishes to go to America, where she dreams a woman does just as she pleases.

For 1794 this protest of sexual domination seemed audacious. Admittedly some discussion of women's rights had taken place; Mary Wollstonecraft's *Vindication of the Rights of Women* had been published in Philadelphia in 1792, and the subject of educaiton for women occasionally served as the topic for a debate. But no one seriously considered any change in the status of women. Why did Rowson choose this play to make her most forthright assertions about the equality of women? Was she, in this hastily written drama, carried along by her own rhetoric about liberty, so that equal rights for women seemed a logical extension of her own argument? That would imply that Rowson was not entirely in control, and such a conclusion seems inconsistent with the Susanna Rowson who so carefully determined her life. A more likely theory is that Rowson constructed her political rhetoric as a vehicle for her feminist assertions.

In fact, a careful reading of the play indicates that she was not as patriotic as she might at first glance have seemed. Fetnah's line about America as a place where a woman does just as she pleases seems incredibly naive. The line assumes perspective when we recall that Fetnah is here dreaming of a country she knows only secondhand. She has never set foot outside Algiers. The American women who do know America speak only of the freedom offered to men: "Columbia's sons be free," and "A boy born in Columbia claims liberty as his birthright." The characters seem unconscious of the irony, but Rowson was not.

Because of her position in a theater company, Rowson was able to have her play performed a number of times. It was first presented on June 30, 1794 and then repeated as a popular stock piece when the company performed in Baltimore and New York.[16] By November, 1795, Rowson had shortened the play for use as an afterpiece.[17] Cutting the play would have intensified the comic elements, which Rowson had made effective by writing parts for particular actors. She wrote the role of the drunken Spaniard Sebastian, for example, for the experienced low comedian Billy Bates, who specialized in pantomime. Sebastian drew applause with a boisterous rhythmic drinking song that lent itself to pantomime. (The music to the play has not been preserved.) Rowson created the other roles for other company members: Ben Hassan was played by the ballet master, William Francis, and the young Moreton played Frederic. The role of Rebecca's son was acted by the son of the Warrells, one of the families in the company. The role of Fetnah, the opinionated and daring slave, was played by Mrs. Marshall, one of Wignell's most talented actresses; and Rebecca and Constant, who in the end discover themselves wife and husband, were played by Mr. and Mrs. Whitlock. Eliza Whitlock, a large, heavy woman, suited the maternal role. Rowson herself played Olivia, Rebecca's daughter. Though Rowson at thirty-two was beginning to grow heavy, she relished the part and spoke with feeling the final lines of the play:

May Freedom spread her benign influence thro' every nation, till the bright Eagle, united with the dove and olive branch, wave high, the acknowledged standard of the world. (3.7.72)

With *Slaves in Algiers*, Rowson entered the mainstream of popular American culture. Americans were demanding new plays; theater managers had to meet those demands. As an actress Rowson found herself in a position to satisfy both the needs of her theater manager and the needs of her audience. She knew what her audience wanted, and she knew the limitations of her company. Though English, she had no trouble adapting herself to the new nationalistic rhetoric, for she believed in democratic ideals as firmly as if she had been a third-generation patriot. She felt no disloyalty in celebrating American freedom, and she was not the only English playwright to do so. In fact,

American audiences liked these English actors and actresses who constituted the majority of the theater companies, and they seemed to
prefer plays by English, rather than American, playwrights.[18] Other
English actors and actresses who wrote plays during this decade were
J. Robinson, a comedian in the Old American Company who wrote
and published *The Yorker's Strategy; or, Banana's Wedding* (1792), a
popular farce; James Fennell, in Rowson's own Philadelphia company,
who wrote *The Advertisement; or, a New Way to Get Married* (1798);
John Beete, an actor in Charleston; and John B. Williamson, for
whom Rowson was later to work.[19]

Though Rowson knew of other Englishmen writing plays for the
American stage, she knew of few other women.[20] The one other
woman who did write a play during this time could not have lent
Rowson much encouragement. Three months before *Slaves in Algiers*
appeared, Anne Kemble Hatton produced *Tammany; or, The Indian
Chief*, in New York. Hatton was one of the numerous Kemble offspring, a sister of Sarah Siddons, and she had arrived in New York
about the same time as Rowson had arrived in Philadelphia. Seizing
upon a local issue, Hatton produced the play under the auspices of
the Tammany Society at the John Street Theater. The play received
praise from the Republicans and the Irish who supported the Tammany Society, but its opening night aroused enough antagonism to
interrupt the performance. Federalist critics objected to its "popular
notions of liberty,"[21] but at least the music merited publication. Thus
Rowson had precedent for writing, as a woman, a topical play on a
nationalistic note, but that did not spare her from criticism.

Although theater reviews as we know them today were almost non-
existent in the 1790s, Rowson's published play elicited one reaction—not so much a review as a political debate. On March 6, 1795,
William Cobbett, the pamphleteer, published *A Kick for a Bite*, com-
menting on a number of subjects and signed "Peter Porcupine," Cobbett's first use of this pseudonym. He addressed the article to Samuel
Harrison Smith, publisher of the *American Literary Review*, and included this castigation of Smith:

. . . what excuse have you for having omitted to take notice of the volumi-
nous productions of the celebrated Mrs. Rowson? Sins of omission were ever
expiable when a lady is in the case; the fair do generally in the long run,
pardon sins of commission, but those of omission they never do. Indeed, Sir,
it was giving them but a pitiful idea of your gallantry, to slip by without
casting a single glance at our American Sappho.[22]

Cobbett then offered his "Review on the roma-drama-poetic works of
Mrs. Susanna Rowson of the New Theatre, Philadelphia." Since space
did not permit him to analyze all of her performances, he wrote that
he must content himself with extracts from *Slaves in Algiers*, which
"may be looked upon as a criterion of her style and manner."

William Cobbett, an Englishman, had spent a few years in France
before emigrating to Philadelphia at the same time Rowson arrived.
During his fourteen months in Delaware as a teacher of French, he
had cultivated an animosity toward things American. He had returned to Philadelphia the same month that the New Theater opened
and had seen Rowson in several productions there. He had read her
books and had seen her "poetical address," "The Standard of Liberty,"
performed in Baltimore.

Rowson epitomized all that Cobbett abhorred in women; her role
as actress made her life public and her writings sought to pass her
ideas on to others. When she went so far as to announce from the
Philadelphia stage the superiority of women over men, Cobbett's ire
would not be contained. Though he protested against her figures of
speech and her grammar, his real objection was clearly her feminism.
He attacked Rowson's vanity for claiming women's equality with
men. As for the couplet from the epilogue, "Women were born for
universal sway / Men to adore, be silent, and obey," he asserted,
"Sentiments like these could not be otherwise than well received in a
country, where the authority of the wife is so universally acknowledged." He anticipated, he said, a House of Representatives constituted entirely of women. To discredit Rowson personally, he
intimated the adulterous behavior of people in the theater.

Cobbett's second main objective was to the patriotic language of
the play. Cobbett was an arch-Federalist, and this attack on Rowson's
democratic principles anticipated his attacks on the Republican Mathew Carey and others. Cobbett claimed to disbelieve in what he
called Rowson's sudden conversion to republicanism. Her use of the
word *liberty* particularly rankled:

Is not the sound of Liberty, glorious Liberty! heard to ring from one end of
the continent to the other? . . . What else is heard in the senate, the pulpit,
the jail, the parlour, the kitchen, and the cradle?[23]

Rowson thus became one of the first of an impressive list of Cobbett's
pamphlet targets, which included Benjamin Rush, Thomas Paine,

Benjamin Franklin, Albert Gallatin, Edmund Randolph, and James Monroe. Abigail Adams described Cobbett as "low and vulgar as a fishwife,"[24] and Nathaniel Hawthorne spoke of "the ferocity of the true bloodhound of literature—such as Swift, Churchill, or Cobbett—which fastens upon the throat of the victim, and would fain drink his life-blood."[25] But Rowson, like so many of Cobbett's later targets, had a reputation and a popular following, so it did not take long for a defender to appear.

John Swanwick (1740–1798), congressman from Pennsylvania, published his first defense of Rowson and attack on Cobbett in a pamphlet entitled *A Rub from Snub: A Cursory Epistle: Addressed to Peter Porcupine Containing Glad Tidings for the Democrats and A Word of Comfort to Mrs. Rowson.* As a politician with literary interests, Swanwick had written a number of pamphlets and was well acquainted with Rowson and her works. He sized up Cobbett accurately. "This 'review,' as you term it, appears to be merely an expletive, in order to swell your pamphlet to a more respectable bulk. . . ." Swanwick then returned Cobbett's fire with vindictiveness. He called Cobbett "Mr. Hedge-Hog" and defined him as an ass with prickly skin. He denied Cobbett's qualifications as critic and faulted him for waiting for months after the play's first production. Despite Swanwick's good intentions toward Rowson, his counter to Cobbett's attack on Rowson's feminism suggests even Swanwick did not take the statements in her play seriously. He described some of Rowson's comments as only fun:

merely a sally of humor, intended to create a smile, and not to enforce a conviction of women's superiority. In all polite circles (with which I presume you [William Cobbett] have little intercourse) the superiority is always ascribed to women, when in fact they may possess an inferiority.[26]

But Swanwick by no means shared Cobbett's view of woman as drudge. He believed that the distinctions between the sexes were based on "customs and manners," and that a male education would qualify a woman for "all the duties of a man."

Swanwick also defended Rowson's praise of "charity, friendship, and philanthropy" as attributes of the American character. He confessed that he did not know Rowson personally and hoped she would not find his vindication officious or presumptuous but would take it "as a candid eulogium to the intrinsic merit of works which we cannot sufficiently applaud." He then recommended that Rowson ignore

Cobbett, not condescend to reply to him, and should she "indulge her audience with another epilogue at her next benefit I would particularly advise her not to mention . . . [Cobbett's] name."

As for Cobbett, Swanwick warned him against future attacks on Rowson in terms of suggesting Swanwick had heard of Rowson's temper:

Should you provoke the vengeance of Rowson, you would stand no more chance than insects beneath a discharge of thunderbolts. Whippets that seize the heels of horses often get their brains kicked out.[27]

Indeed Rowson had a fierce temper when provoked, but just now she contained her anger. She knew that such publicity as both Cobbett and Swanwick provided could only benefit sales of her novels and plays as well as box office sales at the New Theater. She knew too that to condescend to become a pamphleteer would invite more criticism, perhaps from those more respected than William Cobbett. And so, at least publicly, she withheld her temper.

In keeping with her public image of a dignified and morally upright actress, she restrained her reply, limiting it to a single defense in the preface of her upcoming novel, *Trials of the Human Heart:*

It is with reluctance I find myself obliged to remark that the literary world is infested with a kind of loathsome reptile, of the class of non-descripts, for it cannot be ranked, with propriety among either authors or critics, not possessing the qualifications necessary to form either, and being in itself remarkable for nothing but its noxious qualities: its only aim is to prevent the success of any work of genius; and swelling with envy, should the smallest part of public favour, be conferred on another, spits out its malignant poison, in scurrility and detraction. One of these noisome reptiles, has lately crawled over the volumes, which I have had the temerity to submit to the public eye. I say *crawled* because I am certain it has never penetrated beyond the title of any.[28]

Rowson called all of Cobbett's allegations "false and scurrilous," and to demonstrate how her loyalties had grown "equally attached" to both Great Britain and the United States, she used the metaphor of a family:

The unhappy dissentions affected me in the same manner as a person may be imagined to feel, who having a tender lover, and an affectionate brother who are equally dear to her heart . . . sees them engaged in a quarrel with, and fighting against each other, when let whichsoever party conquer, she cannot be supposed insensible to the fate of the vanquished. (xviii–xix)

Rowson remained silent about Cobbett's attacks on her feminism. To proclaim female superiority in the context of a play was one thing, but to defend that proclamation in the clear light of a preface was another. The dramatic work had served its purpose. She had stated her position and had gained publicity by being attacked and defended.

Cobbett, however, loved the fray, and he entered the arena again in May with a reply to Swanwick entitled "A Bone to Gnaw for the Democrats. Part II."[29] He prefaced this essay by saying that readers would not get from him "an answer to citizen Scrub" because "I hate controversy more, if possible, than I do sans-culottism." Though most of the pamphlet ridiculed Swanwick, Cobbett's only reference to Rowson was the protest that his motive had been to "deliver her unfortunate play, *The Slaves in Algiers*, from obscurity."

The following year Swanwick published two other pamphlets condemning Cobbett, *British Honour and Humanity; or the Wonders of American Patience* and *A Roaster; or a Check to the Progress of Political Blasphemy intended as a brief reply to Peter Porcupine.*[30] The latter contained no reference to Rowson, and the first one briefly alluded to Cobbett's "furious attack" on *Slaves in Algiers*.

Other Plays. So ended Rowson's only venture into politics. She did not like the strident voice of pamphlet politics and in the future avoided such controversy. She refused, however, to let Cobbett prevent her from writing plays about political events. Her next play dealt with the so-called Whisky Rebellion, an outbreak in southwestern Pennsylvania which occurred in the fall of 1794, as farmers resisted the federal excise tax. The play was entitled *The Volunteers*. In defiance of Cobbett's objection to her use of the word *liberty*, Rowson wrote lyrics that exuberantly celebrated liberty. The volunteers, that is, the militia called by Washington to enforce the law, sing of love, of the joys of simple frontier life, and of their American freedom.[31]

For this play, or "musical entertainment" as it was described, Rowson collaborated with Wignell's comanager of the New Theater, Alexander Reinagle.[32] Rowson had warmed to Reinagle as soon as they met and discovered they both came from Portsmouth, England. Six years older that she, Reinagle had come to the United States in

1786, while Rowson was entering the world of the English theater. Reinagle had lived first in New York, teaching pianoforte, harpsichord, and violin. He had moved to Philadelphia in 1786 and since then had been sponsoring "city concerts" and giving music lessons. His connections with leading Philadelphia families had greatly promoted the theater since 1791, when he became the theater comanager. Reinagle had found his theater responsibilities gratifying, for he and Wignell shared a belief in the importance of music on the public stage. Together they were offering the Philadelphia public more musical productions than any other theater, and Reinagle was writing music for all productions as well as directing the twenty-five member orchestra. Rowson responded enthusiastically to Reinagle's love of music and found him a demanding but dignified man with whom to work. He welcomed her eagerness to write musical numbers, and very shortly after the company opened they began to collaborate. By mid-March they had produced the popular "America, Commerce, and Freedom," for the ballet pantomime *The Sailor's Landlady*. Then they wrote a new song for an old work, "A Soldier is the Noblest Name," for the O'Keefe opera *The Highland Reel*. By mid-April when Rowson approached Reinagle with her proposed *Slaves in Algiers*, they were experienced collaborators. Although today these numbers are the only extant songs by Rowson and Reinagle, the pair undoubtedly wrote others. Reinagle constantly searched for more musical material, and he found in Rowson a company member who could write lyrics as readily as she could sing them.

The score remains the only extant part of *The Volunteers*, and it is located in the Library of Congress. It consists of thirteen songs by Rowson and Reinagle and one borrowed from a London song published three years earlier. The Rowson/Reinagle numbers are of a sort that would easily become popular with theater audiences, light, simple melodies in major keys. This duet opens the ballad-opera:

> *Thomas:* Here beneath our lowly Cott
> Tranquil peace and pleasure dwell
> If contented with out lot
> Smiling Joy can grace excel.
>
> *Jemima:* Natures wants are all supply'd
> Food and raiment, house and fire,
> Let others swell the courts of pride
> This is all that we require.

> *Thomas:* When day just glimmers in the east
> Blythesome we leave our humble bed
> Chearful at night partake the feast
> By bounteous nature kindly spread.
>
> *Jemima:* We'll chearful our endeavours blend,
> Yes ev'ry future moment spend
>
> *Both:* To make your time pass cheerily
> To make your time pass cheerily.

Other songs include delicate love lyrics, humorous numbers, and a lively soldier's song.

Another play of Rowson's, *The Female Patriot; or, Nature's Rights*, was performed by the company some time in 1794.[33] No known copy exists, and indeed the play, like most at the time, may never have been printed. The title suggests that Rowson continued her feminist theme in this play, which she based on Philip Massinger's *The Bondman*, keeping many of Massinger's characters. Massinger's popular Jacobean comedy, like *Slaves in Algiers*, concerns a slave revolt and a female hero. *The Female Patriot* apparently included no music. For her benefit night on June 17, 1796, Rowson wrote another play, *The American Tar, or the Press Gang Defeated.*[34] As with *Slaves in Algiers* and *The Volunteers*, this "ballet," as it was subtitled, was based on a current event, a "recent fact at Liverpool." For the music Rowson collaborated with Raynor Taylor, another emigrant musician, previously music director at Sadler's Wells Theatre in London, and a friend and teacher of Alexander Reinagle.[35] As this production called for little actual acting, Rowson wrote parts for both her husband and her husband's sister, Charlotte—a treat for them, since William Rowson seldom performed on the Philadelphia stage, and Charlotte, young and not greatly talented, usually performed only minor roles. William sang "Independent and Free," a number that became quite popular. *The American Tar* was probably an adaptation from a work by Jacob Morton and was probably never published; no known copy exists today. Rowson sold or gave the rights to this play to the actor and manager-partner of the Old American Company, John Hodgkinson, who produced and performed in the play at the opening of the Park Street Theater on January 29, 1798.[36]

When Rowson moved to Boston she continued her dramatic writing in addition to her writing of fiction. Her comedy, *Americans in England; or Lessons for Daughters*, was first performed on April 19,

1797.[37] Only the list of characters remains to tantalize the dramatic historian today. The English characters' names imply their English eccentricities: Courtland, Frolic, Snap, Waiter, Jack, and Arabella Acorn; while the American characters convey sturdy American qualities: Ezekiel Plainly, Horace Winship, Jemima Winship. Rowson herself played the roles of Mrs. Ormsby and Jemima Winship, the heroine, and she again wrote roles for her husband and sister-in-law. The title and list of characters suggest that the play praised the United States through a strong-minded woman, a daughter of Columbia, played by the author. The Boston audience received the play enthusiastically, delaying Rowson's delivery of the epilogue with their applause and following her exit with three "distinct plaudits," according to an anonymous review in the *Massachusetts Mercury* of April 21, 1797.[38] Despite this reception Rowson made no money from the production, so she gave the rights to John Hodgkinson, who renamed it *The Columbia Daughter: or, Americans in England* and used it for his benefit at the New York Mt. Vernon Gardens Theater on September 10, 1800.

Song Lyrics. Rowson's Philadelphia musical contacts provided her with a ready introduction into the musical circles of Boston, and within a short time after her arrival there she had met the musicians of the day, again English and European immigrants: Samuel Arnold, Oliver Holden, James Hewitt, Peter Van Hagen, and Gottlieb Graupner. Of these, Hewitt, Arnold, and Graupner came from the theater; Peter Van Hagen taught music both at his own music school and later for Rowson's Boston Academy while operating a music store with his son. Rowson soon began writing lyrics for the songs of these composers and for others. She wrote a variety of songs, love songs, sea chanties, and patriotic numbers.

When Benjamin Carr, whom she had met in Philadelphia, came to Boston in 1797 or 1798, he composed the music for Rowson's "In Vain is the Verdure of Spring," a love song published in Philadelphia in 1798. This song typifies her pastoral love songs:

> Restrain'd from the sight of my dear
> No object with pleasure I see
> Tho' thousands around me appear
> The world's but a desert to me.
> In vain is the verdure of spring
> The trees look so blooming and gay

> The Birds as they whistle and sing
> The Birds as they whistle and sing
> Delight not when William's away. . . .[39]

This song achieved some popularity and was reprinted in several collections.

Many of Rowson's love songs, however, are of a different sort and do not convey the sweet innocence of "Willy of the Dale" or "In Vain is the Verdure of Spring." Often they reflect an impertinence: "I Never Will Be Married, I'd Rather Be Excus'd." Typical of these is "He is Not Worth the Trouble:

> Ye Maidens then beware of men,
>   They're all alike believe me,
> They all proceed on Damon's plan
>   And flatter to deceive ye.
> Then let not love your senses blind,
> For should you meet one to your mind,
> And marry! ten to one you'll find,
> He is not worth the trouble.[40]

Carr also wrote the music for Rowson's "The Little Sailor Boy," which he took back with him to Philadelphia to have Rowson's ex-colleagues in the Chestnut Street Theater company sing in Philadelphia, Baltimore, and New York. Benjamin Carr printed and sold it as sheet music as did his father, Joseph Carr, in Baltimore, and their fellow musician and music publisher, James Hewitt, in New York. This song falls somewhere between Rowson's love songs and her sea chanties, being a love song about a boy away at sea. The lyrics might have been prompted either by her half brother William or by her husband's natural son, whom she raised. The poignancy of the lyrics and the simple tune made the song popular in east coast cities and towns. Even in this maritime love song Rowson inserted a word about tyranny:

> Oh may he never be compell'd
> To cringe to pow'r or mix with Slaves;
> May love and Peace his steps attend,
> Each future hour be wing'd with Joy,
> Like that when I again shall meet
> My much lov'd little Sailor Boy.[41]

Love songs, however, were not Rowson's favorite genre. She excelled at sea chanties, with rollicking, quick-moving rhythms and boisterous lyrics, atypical of women's poetry. "America, Commerce, and Freedom" was one of the most popular of this genre, written originally for the ballet pantomime, *The Sailor's Landlady* in 1794. The third stanza reflects the sailor's language and attitudes Rowson had picked up from her family and family friends:

> Our prizes sold, the chink we share,
> And gladly we receive it;
> And when we meet a brother tar,
> That wants, we freely give it;
> No freeborn sailor yet had store,
> But cheerfully would lend it;
> And when 'tis gone—to sea for more:
> We earn it but to spend it.
> Then drink round, my boys, 'tis the first of our joys,
> To relieve the distress'd, clothe, and feed 'em;
> 'Tis a duty we share with the brave and the fair,
> In this land of Commerce and Freedom.[42]

Each verse contains a reference to drinking, both by sailors and by their "bonnie lasses," and this song remained popular for years in the New England area.

Chapter Four
American Novels

American Publication of English Novels

Always ambitious, eager to make a name for herself as well as money for her family's support, Susanna Rowson brought her English publications with her to Philadelphia and promptly sought a publisher for two of them. Carefully anticipating her American audience, she selected from six previously published novels two that Americans would receive favorably. She took *Rebecca; or, the Fille de Chambre* to H. & P. Rice and J. Rice & Co. in 1794, and when she traveled with the theater company to Baltimore the same year, she persuaded George Keating, a bookseller in that city, to publish yet another edition. The book sold well, and two more editions appeared in Baltimore in 1795, the last year Rowson worked there as an actor. After Rowson moved to Boston and opened a school, editions were printed there in 1814, 1831, and 1832, and the book remained in booksellers' catalogs for the next forty years.[1] The 1814 edition included a new autobiographical introductory chapter in which Rowson confirmed the authenticity of the American sequence in the novel and rather charmingly reminisced about its composition.

Rebecca appealed to American audiences as it had not to English. Frank Luther Mott includes this novel in his list of "better sellers," American books of nearly best-seller popularity, one of only twenty books in this decade that he feels deserves the distinction.[2] As the story of the heroine's coming of age, an initiation novel in which the heroine achieves maturity and knowledge of the world, *Rebecca* appealed to citizens of a youthful country. At a time when cartoons and literature pictured the young United States as a woman cast off by a cruel and abusive parent, this story of a young woman abandoned by both her real mother and by her female patron aroused nationalistic interest. The heroine has a proud and independent demeanor. Ultimately she is reconciled with her long-lost mother and wins her blessing. The fifty-page interlude in which the heroine lives in

Massachusetts and suffers hardships during the American Revolution added further interest for American readers.

Rowson's second American publication proved even wiser, for *Charlotte Temple* caught the attention of the American audience immediately. Showing the shrewd business sense that characterized her actions in later years, she took this novel to the bookseller and publisher who could most effectively distribute her books, Mathew Carey, at 18 Market Street, Philadelphia. Rowson had learned from her experience with William Lane in London the value of an industrious and successful publisher with a marketing network. Carey's six-year-old business was growing steadily, and he was on his way to becoming one of the most successful publishers of his time. Carey's effective distribution techniques contributed to the popularity of Rowson's novel, and soon it became his best-selling stock. The first edition sold so well that Carey issued a second edition the same year.

Before *Charlotte Temple*, best-selling authors in America had been Goldsmith, Sterne, Fielding, and Smollett.[3] Rowson's novel, written by a woman who eventually lived in the United States for thirty-one years, with its American setting, became the first "American best seller."[4] R. W. G. Vail has called *Charlotte Temple* "the most popular of all American novels" before *Uncle Tom's Cabin*, and he documented 161 editions, fifty-nine in New York, thirty-nine in Philadelphia, twelve in Hartford. Even relatively small towns printed their own editions. Six editions were printed in England, one in France, one in Germany, and one in Ecuador.[5]

In 1797 Mathew Carey issued a third edition, changing the original title, *Charlotte, A Tale of Truth*, to *Charlotte Temple*, by which the book became known. Other later titles included *A History of Charlotte Temple, founded on fact*, (several editions), *The Lamentable History of the Beautiful and Accomplished Charlotte* (Philadelphia, 1860, 1865), and *The Cheap Edition of Charlotte Temple* (Boston, 1846). For the next one hundred years Rowson was identified as being "with the New Theater, Philadelphia" even though she left Philadelphia in 1796, the theater burned to the ground in 1798, and the author herself died in 1824.[6] Various nineteenth-century editions added illustrations, including portraits of Charlotte and illustrated scenes from the novel. Some even included scenes not from the novel, such as a young woman leaning against a tombstone. The plate depicting Charlotte's gravestone in Trinity Churchyard first appeared in a New York edition of 1840.

Many of these editions played upon the "Charlotte cult." By the mid-nineteenth century thousands of readers believed in the literal truth of the novel, as newspapers printed portraits of Charlotte and popular lore identified her house in New York on the corner of Pell and Doyers Streets.[7] Charlotte's gravesite in Trinity Churchyard became the object of pilgrimages for the romantic. The original gravestone was said to have read "Charlotte Stanley" and to have been stolen in 1848 when Trinity was being rebuilt. When a worker noticed the missing marker, he ordered a new stone cut with the name "Charlotte Temple."[8] As late as 1903 people could recall the power exercised by Rowson's short novel, as in this contribution to the *New York Evening Post*:

When I was a boy the story of Charlotte Temple was familiar in the household of every New Yorker. The first tears I ever saw in the eyes of a grown person were shed for her. In the churchyard are graves of heroes, philosophers, and martyrs, whose names are familiar to the youngest scholar, and whose memory is dear to the wisest and best. Their graves, tho' marked by imposing monuments, win but a glance of curiosity, while the turf over Charlotte Temple is kept fresh by falling tears.[9]

Vail reported in 1932 that he purchased copies of *Charlotte Temple* readily and that the book was being used in college American literature courses.

Although Rowson would have felt pleased with the long-lasting success of her novel, she would not have liked the liberties that publishers and writers were to take with the book after her death. The 1865 edition published by Barclay and Co. in Philadelphia, for example, omitted her name altogether and identified the story as an American legend. This edition reduced the novel to twenty-one pages but added three more chapters than the original.[10] At least one dramatic version of the novel also took advantage of its popularity and plagiarized freely. In 1899 Charlotte Pixley Plumb published *Charlotte Temple, a Historical Drama*, a play which freely omitted much of the novel's plot, added and deleted characters, and changed both action and dialogue.[11] The first act opens in Charlotte's home in New York, reducing the school scenes and elopement to a brief "Prologue." By the end of act 2, Charlotte is raving mad, though she has not given birth, and in fact, the audience cannot be quite sure she has ever lost her virginity. The third act contains far more melodrama than the

original novel, with Belcour and Montraville fighting offstage, Belcour and LaRue planning to escape together, and Charlotte ceasing
her mad ranting long enough to recite the Lord's Prayer and die. The
play emphasizes the conflict between Britain and the colonies and
contains references to Washington and Hancock, makes proper villains of the British, with appropriately disparaging comments about
the American colonists. Nowhere does Rowson's name appear.[12] The
play demonstrates a reworking of Rowson's material to please late
nineteenth-century American taste.

Why did this novel, in many ways a conventional seduction story,
achieve such popularity? A number of critics have speculated about
this phenomenon. Francis Halsey in 1905 attributed the novel's popularity to its literal truth, its moral lessons, and its delineation of
"every-day human emotions."[13] In 1907 Lillie Deming Loshe ascribed
Charlotte Temple's popularity to its sensationalism, its simplicity, and
its directness.[14] In 1917 Carl Van Doren returned to the question of
the truth of the novel, which he found the reason for its popularity.[15]
In 1948 Alexander Cowie attributed its success to its "sincerity and
power," which affected even modern readers.[16] Leslie Fiedler based its
success largely on the plot, and he claimed that women enjoyed the
novel because they liked images of themselves as long-suffering martyrs victimized by male lust.[17] Clara and Rudolph Kirk thought that
the book's claim to an actual family scandal as well as its moral precepts made it appropriate to eighteenth- and nineteenth-century
readers. The morality, sentimentality, and melodrama, however, appealed as easily to a modern audience and justified a new edition in
1964.[18] More recently critics have speculated about the "hidden message" in *Charlotte Temple*. Feminist critics believe Rowson was teaching her readers to avoid Charlotte's helplessness and become strong
like Julia Franklin and that readers consciously or unconsciously appreciated this message.

All the factors mentioned here undoubtedly contributed to the success of *Charlotte Temple*. Significant too is the effect of Rowson's ma-
nipulation of the eighteenth-century English seduction novel in a way
that spoke particularly to a nineteenth-century American audience.
Rowson's was one of the earliest American novels to use what became
the conventional seduction theme, the father-daughter relationship
disturbed by the daughter's lover. This conflict appears frequently in
American literary periodicals such as *Godey's Lady's Book*, *Graham's*,
and lesser periodicals from 1800 to 1850. In all of these short stories

the heroines are graceful, virtuous, innocent, and usually beautiful. The fathers, like Mr. Temple, dote upon their daughters. The lover interrupts this relationship, and the heroine always gets pregnant and bears a baby that sometimes dies shortly after birth. Like *Charlotte Temple*, the stories concentrate on the daughters and their problems and teach that daughters should obey their parents and that parents should not overly repress their children.[19]

A number of factors in *Charlotte Temple* characterize it as a nineteenth-century rather than an eighteenth-century work. First, Charlotte's helplessness typifies the Victorian view of woman. The frailty she exhibits in her seasickness suggests the fashionable poor health so often mentioned in nineteenth-century literature. The sentimentality of her deathbed scene, with Charlotte surrendering her infant to her father, appealed to a culture that sentimentalized death and idealized motherhood. Ironically, this novel succeeded in part because it promoted ideas Rowson did not believe in.

Trials of the Human Heart

For whatever reasons, *Charlotte Temple* brought Rowson a degree of fame during her lifetime. But never content to rest on past achievements, Rowson set to work immediately on another novel and by 1796 published *The Trials of the Human Heart*. This novel was the first Rowson wrote in America. She published it in four volumes by subscription, and it was printed by two Philadelphia firms, Wrigley and Berriman, and Mountford, Bioren Co. Sales were distributed among several booksellers, Carey, Rice, Campbell, Ormrod and Young, and Rowson sold copies herself, but only one edition was published.[20] Rowson had not sold a novel by subscription since her very first work, and publication by subscription had passed out of favor in the United States as it had in England. But because she felt less sure of herself in this country, and because she found an influential patron, she chose to publish *Trials* by this old method.

Rowson dedicated the book to "Mrs. Bingham," whose name headed the impressive, four-page list of subscribers, including Martha Washington, Mrs. Henry Knox, and members of leading Philadelphia families as well as Wignell, Reinagle, and most of the New Theater Company. The subscribers suggested the influence of Rowson's patron as well as the strength of the author's reputation. Anne Bingham, Rowson's new Philadelphia patron, was in fact a patron of Wig-

nell's theater. At the age of thirty-one, educated, beautiful, and immensely wealthy, she dominated Philadelphia's fashionable circles.
She and her husband William, who had earned a fortune during the
Revolution, had recently built a large mansion on Third Street, with
grounds that created envy among all Philadelphians. Anne Bingham
had taken an interest in the Chestnut Street Theater close to her home
and frequently took large parties to performances there.[21] Rowson felt
proud of her association with a woman so highly regarded, but unfortunately the connection did not last. Shortly after *Trials* appeared,
Anne Bingham requested of Thomas Wignell permission to furnish
and keep a key to her own private box in the theater. When Wignell
refused, she boycotted the theater and led others to do the same.[22]
Rowson lost an influential friend, and the company lost some of its
audience.

Despite Bingham's patronage, *Trials of the Human Heart* proved one
of Rowson's least successful works. Writing in the epistolary form
which she had not used since *Victoria*, Rowson related the story of
Meriel Howard through sixteen years of adventures. Meriel tells her
story in a series of letters to her friend Celia, a resident in the French
convent that Meriel has just left. Meriel returns to England to the
couple she believes to be her parents, only to have her father attempt
to rape her and then succeed in cheating her out of her inheritance.
As a result, Meriel is thrust into the world to care for herself and the
woman she believes to be her mother. Her trials continue for sixteen
years and include a marriage to a man she does not love, before she
finally succeeds in settling down with the love of her life, Frederic
Rainsforth.

The novel contains a number of autobiographical references. Again,
at least one character, like Rowson herself, is the daughter of a retired
naval lieutenant; another character leaves for naval duty from Portsmouth, Rowson's home town; and the heroine, again like the author,
hopes to pursue a writing career. The heroine attends a theater production of *Jane Shore*, a play in Rowson's company's repertoire in Baltimore the summer of 1795, and the heroine also undergoes, as the
author had at the age of five, a terrible storm at sea. Another character reads and praises the novels of Mrs. Bennett, the novelist under
whose direction Rowson had performed at the Edinburgh Theatre. In
addition to these references, the preface to *Trials* contains a detailed
autobiographical description of the main events of Rowson's childhood, inserted as a defense against William Cobbett's attack on the

author's American loyalty. But the novel itself is set in England and contains no references to the United States.

Possibly Rowson's stage experiences, more extensive in Philadelphia than in England, account for the occasional idiomatic flavor of the dialogue in the novel. Meriel's speech, though usually formal, sometimes sounds realistically colloquial. She writes of her first husband Rooksby, for example, "if he is as gallant and tender twelve months hence, I may perhaps, stand a good chance of claiming the flitch of bacon."[23] This everyday phrase was also used as the title of a play with which Rowson may have been familiar. Another character tells Meriel, "absence and salt water are in general a cure for love" (1: 131). And Dolly Pringle uses the exclamation "la, miss," like a comic stage figure.[24] Unfortunately, most characters speak with a stiff formality, regardless of their background or situation.

Although *Trials* bears little structural resemblance to other Rowson works, it does reiterate some of the author's favorite themes. Once again Rowson conveyed her belief in compassion for a "fallen" woman. Any woman in need merits Meriel's attention, regardless of whether Meriel likes her or whether the woman has treated Meriel unjustly. Of her own husband's mistress Meriel writes, "whatever had been her errors, she was now penitent and in distress, ... I did not hesitate in resolving to become her friend" (3:102). In return Meriel receives the support and assistance of other women, again underscoring the value of the friendship of women. In *Trials* this idea is carried further than in the other novels, however, for Meriel seeks aid and comfort of women because of her distrust of men. By the second volume Meriel's experiences have so affected her that she feels she can "never again place a confidence in any man" (2:4), and she resolves "to despise the whole sex; they may wear a semblance of virtue, but the reality of it is foreign to their hearts" (2:6).

Meriel's bitterness extends to social criticism, as *Trials* reflects a view of the world more negative than in any of Rowson's writing except *Sarah*, written in despondency over her marriage. The social world of *Trials* is peopled with fools and cheats. Meriel declares herself sick of the social "parade, shew, and farce":

How tiresome to be plagued with the civil howdye's of fifty . . . who are immensely happy to hear you are well, and would say, with the same *sang froid*, they were immensely sorry if they were told you were dead. (1:53)

But Meriel has resiliency and by volume three bounces back. Though she finds herself repeatedly victimized by both men and women, she remains romantically idealistic and hopeful. She calls herself a "castle builder" and permits her admiration for Rooksby's mother, together with the romantic atmosphere of Oak Hall, the Rooksby family seat, to persuade her to marry a man she does not love.

The themes that might appear especially designed for Rowson's American audience are ideas that run through much of her work, the democratic ideal and the democracy of virtue. An American reader who had seen *Slaves in Algiers* and had heard her American songs might recognize in *Trials* the depiction of the moral inferiority of people of wealth and rank and the corresponding superiority of virtue in people at the bottom of the social scale. Another peculiarly American characteristic of the work is its portrayal of the motherless daughter that appeared in a number of novels during the period of the young republic.[25] Meriel's mother is a selfish, cruel, and abusive parent, yet Meriel endeavors to please her, sacrifices her inheritance to pay her expenses, in short, stops at nothing to try to please her, all to no avail. When her mother dies, Meriel's tribulations continue until the very end when she discovers a new set of parents and lives happily ever after.

Despite this thematic similarity to her previous works, *Trials* did not represent an artistic step forward for the author. Its weaknesses are many and indicate the haste with which it was written, at a time when Rowson was acting, writing for the stage, and handling a difficult husband. Indeed, that she found time for fiction at all attests to her remarkable energy. Perhaps the central problem with the book is its episodic structure. The novel spans sixteen years, all of which are covered in letters from Meriel to her friend Celia, still resident at the French convent where Meriel once lived. Meriel's adventures must astound a woman sheltered in a quiet religious retreat, for Meriel encounters an incredible array of misfortunes. She narrowly escapes an incestuous rape and an elopement with a married man, suffers the loss of her fortune and the loss of her true love through deceit, grows so impoverished that she is tempted by prostitution, feels the humility of enforced unemployment, marries a man she does not love, loses her children, bears up through her husband's adultery, and lives through a shipwreck. The title suggests the novel's episodic structure, for Meriel's trials connect the whole. At times the novel seems picaresque, though we meet many of the same characters repeatedly, and in the end the author ties together events and characters and resolves any remaining conflicts. The speed with which incidents occur so diminishes the credibility of both characters and events that ultimately the reader scarcely cares about either. When Meriel in the end learns that the couple she believed were her parents were merely an aunt and uncle, a reader feels the discovery is merely superfluous and cannot share Meriel's relief that her attack was merely attempted rape, not incest. Rowson's failure to eliminate some incidents and to create a sense of meaning for the reader makes her seem out of control of her material.

Another weakness in the novel is in the characterization. Although most Rowson characters are relatively flat and undeveloped, often more reminiscent of allegory than of drama,[26] in *Trials* this fault is compounded by the length of the work (the book runs over six hundred pages) and by the complexity of the rapidly moving plot. The reader encounters one trite character after another. Meriel grows dull simply because she encounters so many villains and desperate situations, though at moments she comes through as realistic and admirable.

In her best scenes Meriel demonstrates the strength of other Rowson heroines, able to overcome all odds by relying on common sense and intelligence. Despite her romantic lapses, such as her foolish marriage to Rooksby, she epitomizes Rowson's faith in the power of reason. When her employer, Mr. Larcus, attempts to seduce her, for example, she simply threatens to tell his wife about his affair with another woman. Meriel also displays an admirable lack of sentimentality. Though forced to earn a living as a milliner, she refuses to lie and flatter in order to hold her job:

I cannot flatter, I cannot tell a woman whom age, and other natural defects, have rendered extremely plain, that a full dress cap with artificial flowers, small handkerchief, and all the gay trappings that belong to the smiling season of eighteen, will become her face and figure; and yet this is a very necessary ingredient in the composition of a milliner. (2:58)

Rowson always maintained that honesty repaid any loss in social or financial consequences.

Meriel also seems more human than other Rowson heroines. She experiences sexual attraction for more than one man and once even for a married man, though she knows her merely average looks do not arouse reciprocal feeling. She also admits to being proud. She seems quite believably human when she refuses to partake of cake and wine in the kitchen with the servants or when she refuses an offer of money from her patronizing brother. She also lives well past the period usually permitted heroines of sentimental novels, about whom we hear no more after their marriage. When *Trials* ends, Meriel is in her thirties, widowed and worldly-wise. Though she finally marries the man she first loved, both she and her lover approach their marriage with an understanding of the world as it really is.

Why did Rowson write this book? In addition to her practical need for income, she sought to improve the public image of actresses by establishing her name in Philadelphia as a reputable instructor of morality for women. But the book did not bring her the acclaim she sought, and within months of its appearance, she moved on to Boston.

Reuben and Rachel; or, Tales of Old Times

While expanding her repertoire of dramatic roles and writing songs, Rowson continued, after coming to Boston, to write fiction. Her next novel anticipated the textbooks she would soon write in her new career as teacher and headmistress. It was called *Reuben and Rachel, or Tales of Old Times* and was published in 1798 by Manning & Loring in Boston. As in her earlier novels, she sought in this work to entertain and instruct, this time enlarging her didactic purpose to include lessons in history:

When I first started the idea of writing Tales of Old Times, it was with a fervent wish to awaken in the minds of my young readers a curiosity that might lead them to the attentive perusal of history in general, but more especially the history of their native country. It has ever been my opinion, that when instruction is blended with amusement, the youthful mind receives and retains it almost voluntarily.[27]

Rowson completed the novel after she had opened her Boston school, by which time she had decided to write a whole series of texts for the formal education of young women. Since most such books were written solely for boys, she would write especially for girls. *Reuben and Rachel* thus surveys in fictional form the history of Western civilization, including many female characters to interest and to serve as examples for young women readers.

The book spans almost three hundred years and takes place in a half-dozen countries, but it maintains thematic unity and narrative clarity. The main theme is democracy, epitomized in the discovery of America, first by Columbus and then by his descendants, Reuben and Rachel. The book traces the movement of democracy from east to west, beginning with fifteenth-century Spanish explorers who plunder and pillage. Christopher Columbus, a brave adventuring hero, seeks and finds a new and better world. Then the narrative moves to sixteenth-century England, where the descendants of Columbus find themselves enmeshed in court intrigues. Next the story moves to seventeenth-century America, with the first English settlers and American Indians; and finally a modern Reuben and Rachel become citizens of the United States. Rowson selected her incidents carefully in this rather awesome undertaking, frequently condensing large segments of time but always keeping characters, time, and place clear in the reader's imagination.

Rowson combined the teachings familiar to a reader of her previous fiction with the historical subject matter that would later serve as basis for some of her textbooks, thus making this novel a transition between her fiction and her pedagogical work. The theme of filial obedience is drawn from previous novels, while the larger view of the history of mankind, with national struggles for power, moves Rowson out of the domestic novel and into a larger worldview. She was preparing for a career in which she would do more than teach girls to escape seduction and maintain their reputations; she was preparing to devote her life to teaching young women the study of history, with the rise and fall of empires and the conquests for gold and power.

Throughout the book the author constantly sought to interest and instruct her female audience. As she would later do in her "Female Biographies," she sketched portraits of admirable women, such as the first Rachel Dudley, who accompanies her man into battle (1:161). Another character tells her daughter how to be a woman:

We must summon all our fortitude to brave even hardship and danger without shrinking. We are women it is true, and ought not to forget the delicacy of our sex; but real delicacy consists in purity of thought, and chastity of words and actions; not in shuddering at an accidental blast of wind, or increasing the unavoidable evils of life by affected weakness and timidity. (1:113)

The character of Rachel, a prototypical "American girl," also appeals to readers, more than many other of the author's heroines. As another of Rowson's unmothered daughters, she not merely survives adventures thrust upon her, but she initiates actions and makes independent decisions. She is self-confident and has little regard for public censure. A few years after this novel Rowson's texts would assert in even plainer terms the equality of which women were capable.

Published four years after the attack by William Cobbett, *Reuben and Rachel* indicates how Americanized Rowson had become. In many of her novels she had denigrated the idea of wealth and rank as indications of merit, but in *Reuben and Rachel* she proclaimed this idea as American. When Reuben and Rachel suddenly inherit English titles and estates, they renounce their titles and vow to use the money for the good of others. Reuben finds titles useless:

[They] should by no means be introduced into a young country, where the only distinction between man and man should be made by virtue, genius and education. Our sons are true-born Americans, and while they strive to make that title respectable, we wish them to possess no other. (2:363)

Rowson's textbooks would end on a similar note, celebrating America and its democratic virtues.

Reuben and Rachel also reflects Rowson's growing interest in her new country and its possibilities for literature. She described seventeenth-century American settlements, albeit in sentimentalized terms, and eighteenth-century rural Philadelphia. And she included as characters American Indians, neither as idealized noble savages nor as Gothic fiends, but as realistic humans with both vices and virtues. Since Rowson had no firsthand experience with Indian speech, she romanticized it with allusions to nature and the Great Spirit. Her dialogue did represent, however, an attempt at realism.

This novel appealed to audiences much more than did *Trials of the Human Heart* and even more than Rowson's later novels set in England. The book appeared in booksellers' catalogs until 1819 in New Haven, New York, Philadelphia, and Salem. A second edition appeared in London in 1799, published by William Lane.[28]

Sarah; or, the Exemplary Wife

The last novel published during Susanna Rowson's lifetime was *Sarah; or, the Exemplary Wife*, which first appeared serially as *Sincerity* in the *Boston Weekly Magazine* from June 4, 1803 to June 30, 1804. *Sarah* holds interest for a modern reader both because it has autobiographical significance and because it differs markedly from Rowson's other novels and from conventional novels of the time.

An autobiographical reading of *Sarah* must be approached carefully, but the author claimed in the preface that many scenes were "drawn from real life." She distanced herself, perhaps to protect her reputation, by adding that the scenes occurred "in another hemisphere, and the characters no longer exist,"[29] but even her nineteenth-century biographer Elias Nason, who sought to present the author in the best light possible, admitted that much of this novel paralleled Rowson's own experiences and claimed that the prologue "Do not marry a fool" derived from her own sufferings.[30]

The novel traces the marriage of Sarah and George Darnley. George proves unfaithful, thoughtless, and hostile to every idea his wife holds dear. Sarah herself displays a less than admirable character in the first stages of her marriage. Following in her husband's footsteps, she becomes heedless of their finances and of the company she keeps. When their financial and emotional situations become unbearable, however, Sarah changes. She makes sincere efforts to reconcile with George, becomes frugal, and alters her behavior for the better. Though Sarah suffers from excessive pride, she tries her best to serve George as a dutiful wife, even going off and supporting herself when her husband claims he prefers to live without her. On her own, she tries to earn a living as a lady's companion and governess, suffering trials similar to those of other young Rowson heroines. As lady's companion and governess she travels to Dublin where she is slandered, cheated of her wages, pursued by a libertine, and finally rescued from desperate poverty by a kindly woman. Returning to England, she enjoys a brief period of reconciliation with her reformed husband, but he soon returns to his wanton ways and plunges her again into misery. Sarah adopts and raises her husband's illegitimate child and later meets a man she might have loved and wed, but she dies early, having dignity and respect but without ever having achieved happiness.

Sarah marries George Darnley for convenience, not love, but her pride and sense of moral duty require her to remain married and faithful for the rest of her life. She finds herself unable to effect a separation:

How totally unprotected a married woman is, when separated from her husband; how every one thinks he may insult her with impunity, and no one will take the trouble to defend her, but rather unite in aspersing and depressing her even to the very earth. (182)

It takes all the courage, fortitude, and perseverance she can muster to maintain her virtue and dignity through years of marriage to a man unworthy of her, but she derives satisfaction in knowing that people respect her, even if they have no respect for her husband.

The novel ranks as one of Rowson's longest, but least complicated, almost leisurely paced novels. The straightforward plot unfolds in a series of letters from Sarah to her friend Anne, Anne's letters to her friend Elenor, and a few letters from less-important and more objective characters. The reader thus is provided with several points of view. Sarah's letters relate the action and convey the sense of urgency that often marks epistolary novels. The dialogue, though limited, is often clever and lively, depicting women characters more fully developed than men, but overall the style is uneven. A series of flashbacks early in the work acquaints the reader with Sarah's early life, and then the action moves forward simply and directly.

This novel differs from most eighteenth- or nineteenth-century novels in several ways. The story opens on Sarah's wedding day, the event with which most domestic novels end. The ending, with the heroine's death, differs from endings that offer death as merciful punishment for evil deeds, for Sarah's good life deserves some reward other than the unmitigated suffering she has endured throughout her marriage. The tone, too, differs from many of Rowson's own and other contemporary novels; the lessons in the book are pessimistic, and the comments on marriage unsentimental, almost foreboding.

Rowson offered advice in this novel to older women, women who had married men they neither loved nor respected. Do your duty, she advised, no matter what, but expect no reward. The title character explains why she does not leave her husband until he wishes it:

If I bound myself by a sacred oath at [the time of my marriage], contrary to my own better judgment, to share his fortunes, be they better or worse, I will not now, in opposition to my sense of duty, forsake him in the hour of humiliation. (109)

Sarah does her duty but takes no pleasure in it, so her early death provides a merciful ending for her, though an uncommon end for a novel.

Rowson also offered advice to young, unmarried women, "the

lovely maidens who are now fluttering on the wing of youth and pleasure" (iv). Proceed into marriage slowly and carefully, she cautioned.
Wedding vows bind until death, and a loveless marriage requires en-
durance and forbearance. Sarah feels pressured to marry because she
no longer has parental "protection," and when she tries to live apart
from her husband she finds the social pressure intolerable, but the author regretted that marriage was the only respectable role for a
woman. Sarah's life then is "exemplary" because she endures the marriage dutifully, and also because she serves as a warning to women
who must yet choose to marry.

The novel also makes some poignant comments, again unconven-
tionally, about marriage. Sarah implies that a thinking woman would
find marriage unbearable:

If every married man is so captious, and petulant, so angry at their wives'
only expressing a difference in opinions in the mildest words: I wonder how
any woman can be so passionately attached to them. But, perhaps, that passionate attachment prevents their seeing any fault in them, and they, suppos-
ing all the man, thus idolized, says, does, or thinks is right, never take the
trouble of contradicting him; assent implicitly to his opinions, however absurd, and will not exert their own mental powers to think or decide for
themselves. (43–44)

When she tries to leave her husband, Sarah asserts, "to be treated either like a child, an idiot, or a slave, is what I cannot, will not submit to" (114). At other times Sarah refers to marriage in terms of
"fetters" and "chains," reminiscent of *Slaves in Algiers* and of the images used in Mary Wollstonecraft's *Vindication of the Rights of Women*:

Want of confidence in a husband, is death to the affection of a wife, and
she who is by turns the slave of capricious passion, or the object of contempt
or neglect, if she is possessed of the least degree of delicacy and feeling, must
suffer a bondage more severe than the slave who is chained to the oar. (259)

When the heroine finally meets a man with whom she can converse
and be friends, she contrasts this relationship with her view of most
men:

Your sex, in general, accustom themselves to consider women in so inferior a
light, that they oftener treat us like children and playthings, than intelligent
beings. . . . How gratifying then, was it to my self love, to be considered

by a man of sense and erudition as an equal, and to be conversed with as a rational companion. (258)

As in *A Present to Young Ladies*, Rowson thus objected to a double standard of intellectual expectation. *Sarah* implies that Rowson held high standards for marriage but that her own reality fell far short of her ideal.

Sarah was published in book form, with only minor changes from the serialized version, by Charles Williams of Boston. Numerous well-preserved copies have been located, suggesting that the book did not enjoy the popularity of other Rowson novels, and Vail locates it in only six booksellers' catalogs, in Boston, New Haven, Philadelphia, and Salem.[31]

Charlotte's Daughter; or, The Three Orphans

Charlotte's Daughter, subtitled *A Sequel to Charlotte Temple*, was found in manuscript after Rowson's death, and no evidence exists as to when she wrote it. The novel represents her attempt to capitalize upon the success of *Charlotte Temple*; its action begins some eighteen years after the first book, and its heroine is the daughter of Charlotte Temple. Set in Hampshire, England, the story revolves around three orphans, Lucy Blakeney, who is Charlotte's daughter, Mary Lumly, and Aura Melville, all under the guardianship of the kindly Reverend Matthews. As the three young women come of age, their actions reflect their early upbringing and the educational efforts of their guardian. Mary Lumly reflects the wrong values she learned from her mother when she elopes with a deceitful young man who marries her only to obtain her inheritance and then leaves her. Aura Melville, though penniless, marries a wealthy man attracted by her fine qualities. Lucy Blakeney plans to wed John Franklin but learns just in time that he is her half brother, the son of Montraville, the seducer of Charlotte Temple. While John goes off to India in remorse, Lucy reconciles herself to an unmarried life and opens a school for girls.

Many elements of this book echo *Charlotte Temple*, though in some ways the sequel is better than the first novel. The most noticeable similarity is that the sequel has the rapid pace and conciseness that made *Charlotte Temple* effective. Though the second book is considerable longer and traces three lives instead of one, the narrative moves quickly and coherently. Rowson used more detailed and vivid descriptions in *Charlotte's Daughter* than in *Charlotte Temple*. At Lucy's birthday dinner, for example, family and neighbors feast on "good sirloins of beef," "plumb puddings" [*sic*], and "wine sangaree," while the local folk move and speak in a realistic and sharply delineated scene. Such details give the book a local flavor lacking in *Charlotte Temple*. Recall that the author had never been to New York when she wrote the first book, but when writing the sequel she sharply visualized Hampshire and sections of northern England.

Lucy Temple, as the book became known after the 1842 edition of that title, harks back to the sensationalism of *Charlotte Temple* not with seduction but with narrowly avoided incest. Incest occurred, or threatened, in several late eighteenth-century English novels and had caused a Boston furor over William Hill Brown's *Power of Sympathy* in 1789. But Rowson did not glamorize the crime in *Lucy Temple;* she used it as retribution for the crimes of her parents. Lucy Blakeney and John Franklin are so awed by their father's seduction of Charlotte Temple and by the fact that they nearly married without knowing of their blood relationship, that they both choose lifelong celibacy rather than marriage. They also choose not to see each other, thereby avoiding an intensely emotional, potentially sentimental farewell.

Montraville, the father of Lucy and John, also connects the two books, though in the latter he is known as "Lt. Franklin," having taken his wife's name many years ago. Lieutenant Franklin appears in the later book only briefly, in his deathbed scene, suitably remorseful for the crime of his youth. He learns of his son's intention to marry Charlotte's daughter in time to prevent it before his death. As in *Charlotte Temple*, Rowson relied upon her cousin John Montresor as the basis of the character of Montraville-Franklin. When Lieutenant Franklin is introduced into the book, the reader learns that after spending years abroad in the service of the army, he has returned to England with a large fortune. While abroad, he has married the only daughter of a wealthy man. He has received "royal thanks for his intrepidity," has established himself in an elegant house in Portland Place, and keeps a summer residence in Kent. All of these facts describe Rowson's cousin, who was still living in his Portland Place home when Rowson left England in 1793.

Although the characterization in *Lucy Temple*, as in most Rowson novels, is for the most part one-dimensional, it holds a reader's interest. Mary Lumly first appears as weak and foolish but she surprises the reader with her strength of will and ability to withstand misfortune. Jack Franklin shows a surprising tenderness and kindness. Aura Melville, who verges on too great perfection, displays an occasional temper. And a number of minor characters provide a humor not often found in Rowson's fiction. Mrs. Cavendish secretly takes snuff. Reverend Matthews tricks Lady Mary into laughing at herself by contriving to set before her, when she is particularly hungry, a tempting dish of plain boiled mutton and unmashed turnips. He then has the satisfaction of watching her eat with pleasure the very dish she has called less than nothing for the poor. The book also reflects Rowson's tolerant views on the subject of religious sects, a tolerance that she acquired with age. In 1788 in *The Inquisitor* she portrayed a ranting Methodist minister devoid of Christian charity, but by the time she wrote this book she took a more sympathetic view. In *Lucy Temple* Reverend Matthews admonishes Mary Lumly for thinking ill of Methodists. "There are many roads to the foot of the cross, and whichever may be taken if it is pursued with a pure and upright heart, is safe."[32]

Written in her last years, *Lucy Temple* was the work of Rowson's old age. The book reflects her increased interest in religion, with its clergyman as a main character and its frequent allusions to the Creator and "the Saviour who redeemed" us. Though Rowson often alluded to "the tenets of the protestant religion" in a general way and always espoused a morality based on Christianity, she never before had infused a work of fiction with so many religious allusions. In *An Abridgment of Universal Geography* (1805) the author trivialized differences between Protestant sects, and in *Reuben and Rachel* (1798) a Quaker argued that "a man might be a very good Christian, though he wore a button to his hat, and ruffles to his shirt." Maturity led Rowson to accept religious variety.

As a part of her increased religious interest, Rowson's concern for charitable causes, which led her to join groups like the Boston Fatherless' and Widows' Society, appeared in *Lucy Temple* repeatedly. Still another reflection of her age was her nostalgia for times and places of her youth. *Lucy Temple* details English houses and views of the countryside recalled from the author's past. Rowson even alluded once, rather wistfully, to the British class system. The wedding of Aura Melville is celebrated in the fashion of "the good old times":

when the poor not only looked up to the gentry for protection and friendship, but took a lively interest in their domestic affairs, were depressed at their misfortunes, and proud and happy in the fame and happiness of their patrons. (177)

After years of celebrating the virtues of democracy, in her last days the author permitted herself to daydream about the time of her youth.

The novel contains one other comment atypical of Rowson, one that suggests weariness with struggle and is perhaps tinged with bitterness. In sharp contrast to *Slaves in Algiers* and other works advocating women's independence and rights, Lucy claims that "the great secret of woman's happiness, [is] to enjoy the happiness of others." That is, happiness for women is achieved vicariously and only when they serve the needs of others. Certainly Rowson in her lifetime had not taken her pleasures vicariously nor had she spent a life of sacrifice and duty to others. She had lived her life according to her own choosing, in an effort to gain some degree of fame and fulfill other personal ambitions. But in her later years she took her pleasures where she could find them, particularly in the happiness of her students. This statement, that women should sacrifice themselves to others, is both a nineteenth-century idea and the voice of a tired and aging woman.

More typical of Rowson, and the role model more forcefully presented in this novel, is the character of the independent woman. Rowson created in Lucy Blakeney a woman who chooses not to marry and who, financially independent, selects for herself a career that will bring her satisfaction. Rowson also portrayed woman's independence in this novel in various other ways. The character Julia Franklin, who had attracted Montraville in *Charlotte Temple* with her wit, intelligence, and air of assurance, impresses the reader in this novel with her quiet strength. Once widowed, she encourages her son to go to India even though his doing so leaves her without a "protector," and she goes off to America on her own, to become a prominent landowner. Rowson indirectly advises women to learn their legal rights, when she depicts Mary's foolish surrender of all her inheritance to her husband. And finally, Rowson's independence surfaces in her handling of the old seduction theme. In this last novel she dared break with the sentimental tradition, which requires the death of the seduced and abandoned woman. Mary Lumly suffers the usual seduction, bad marriage, and pregnancy, but she recovers from her madness and rejoins the Matthews family to live out a quiet and relatively happy life. Mary thus contrasts sharply with Victoria and Charlotte Temple and other lesser characters, all of whom suffer the requisite rapid demise as retribution for their moral crime. In *Lucy Temple* Rowson sought to teach the same lessons about sexual behavior that she had offered in all her fiction, but she portrayed a more realistic end.

Richardson and Lord, publishers of Rowson's last works, issued this novel after the author died. The first edition included a "Memoir" of the author, written by Samuel Lorenzo Knapp and first published in the *Boston Gazette* after Rowson's death. This memoir was the first known account of Rowson's life. Knapp's interest in her stemmed in part from his daughter, Caroline, a pupil at Rowson's Boston Academy, and Knapp found much to admire in his daughter's "preceptress." A writer himself, Knapp had read all of Rowson's canon and appreciated her rejection of Gothicism and the Della-Cruscan school. He praised her "delineations" drawn from nature, the easy familiarity of her style, and the morality of her works. He especially admired her education, industry, and charity.

In April 1828 the *American Ladies' Magazine* briefly reviewed *Lucy Temple*. The reviewer attributed a "want of finish" in Rowson's writing to women's failure to "elaborate their literary productions" but nevertheless found the story interesting and well told, a "valuable addition to the library of the young." Book reviews of women's books had changed little over the forty years in which Rowson had been publishing. A woman writing for women could expect cursory acceptance if her work served a didactic purpose and could do no harm, but she could still not expect serious criticism. The following month Rowson's last novel received her only American review by John Greenleaf Whittier in the *Essex Gazette* of Haverhill, Massachusetts. Whittier quoted extensively a passage from the book, and wrote that he liked Rowson's characters, the book's "moral beauty," and its language of nature, but he acknowledged, without specifying, "imperfections" in style and incident.[33]

Perhaps because it appeared as a sequel to *Charlotte Temple*, *Lucy Temple* enjoyed considerable popularity. Vail counted thirty-one editions but believed more had actually been issued.[34] The book deserves a close examination today for its inherent charm and narrative force but also for its significance in the Rowson canon.

Chapter Five

Textbooks, Poetry, and Essays

Educational Writings

When Rowson opened her school and embarked on a new career in education, she did not entirely abandon the writing of fiction, but her main creative energies went into the writing of textbooks. These books hold significance for what they indicate about her schools and pedagogical methods and for what they tell a reader about Rowson's own prejudices and acquaintance with the world.

An Abridgment of Universal Geography. Rowson's first text was a book on geography, one of her favorite academic subjects. Other geography books existed in the early nineteenth century, but none of them suited her adolescent girl students, so to prepare materials for her classes she put together facts from Jedidiah Morse, the American geographer, and from English texts, with information drawn from her own personal knowledge.[1] The result was a successful geography curriculum that friends and parents of her pupils encouraged her to publish. *An Abridgment of Universal Geography, Together with Sketches of History, Designed for the Use of Schools and Academies in the United States* appeared in 1805, published by John West in Boston. The book consisted of 256 pages of geography text proper followed by "Geographical Exercises" and "Historical Exercises" for memorizing. The latter presented capsulated histories to stimulate student interest in the places described. The sections in the geography covered the globe, moving from country to country and then through the United States. Rowson described location and boundaries, topology, resources, climate, industry, government, religion, and the character of the people of each region. She began with Europe because that is where "the human mind has made the greatest progress toward improvement, and there the arts whether of utility or ornament, the sciences both civil and military, have been carried to the greatest perfection."[2]

Rowson stated in the preface her intention of including her own "moral reflections," for a completely objective text would have been unheard of and ill received. Her descriptions of various peoples indicated openly her own values. The section on England, for example, reflected her admiration for the British character, undiminished after twelve years away from her native country:

The English, in their persons, are well sized, regularly featured, with florid complexions; and of all nations the most cleanly. Their marking characteristics are bravery and humanity. An Englishman of good education is allowed to be the most accomplished gentleman in the world; he is however shy, and reserved in his communications. (43)

At the same time she held an equally high regard for her adopted country and its people, and did not miss the chance to encourage her young pupils' positive image of themselves:

The New Englanders are tall, stout, and well built; the women in general elegantly formed, and handsome. The characteristic of both sexes is that humanity and spirit of brotherly love, which cannot behold a fellow creature in distress, without extending the hand of comfort and assistance. They are friendly, hospitable, and well inclined towards strangers; so much so, that few who have resided in New England any considerable time, but quit it with regret, and remember its inhabitants with sentiments of respect and esteem. (181)

A large part of the book is devoted to America, including descriptions of each of its states and territories.

In fact, Rowson showed a decided preference for England, Scotland, and America, where people held dear the virtues she valued: Protestantism, democracy, industry, cleanliness, and good health. She praised other countries to the extent that they demonstrated these values. She noted that the people of Greenland and Iceland were clean, neat, and religious, and that the Swiss were industrious and intelligent. In Norway, she told her students, "the lowest Norwegian peasant [was] an artist, a gentleman, and often a poet" (20). The Scots exercised economy and self-restraint and enjoyed a low crime rate, and though their theology had once been rigidly Calvinistic, by Rowson's time "the doctrine of the modern Scotch divines [was] distinguished by good sense and moderation" (38).

The corollary to such praise is of course that Rowson disliked countries that did not share her values. She did not approve of Catholicism, and so she criticized Catholic countries. France, though possessed of women of wit and vivacity, suffered a "national vanity" that supported women "under misfortunes," and impelled them "to actions, to which true courage [inspired] others" (55). Spain suffered from "indolence" and an excess of clergy but had "little true religion" (82). Italy labored under "lazy" priests and "superstition and oppression" (91), though its artistic accomplishments deserved praise. The Greek Orthodox Church differed little from "popery" in Rowson's eyes because it practiced "idolatrous and superstitious customs" (32).

Part of what Rowson disliked in Catholicism was its religious elitism and church hierarchy which permitted a despotic exercise of clerical power over the laity. Consistent with this view was her antipathy toward tyranny in any form, as expressed in *Slaves in Algiers*. In *An Abridgment of Universal Geography* Rowson criticized Mongolia, Siam, Turkey, Arabia, and other undemocratic countries. She described Arabs as thieves and Turks as narrow-minded, badly educated about the world, and "lazy, even to a proverb, [with] no idea of riding, walking, or taking any kind of exercise, either for health or diversion" (104). *Slaves in Algiers* had also demonstrated this intense prejudice against peoples of the Middle East, both Arabs and Jews. Even the southern parts of the United States did not satisfy the author's democratic standards. Virginia had admirable, influential men who had fought bravely in the Revolution, but these men had not helped educate and raise the standards of the "lower order," who were "ignorant and abject"(219). North Carolina neglected education of its children. But if Rowson disapproved of religious hierarchy and tyranny as undemocratic, she reserved her strongest ire for the practice of growing rich on the sale of human slaves. Of this offense various Europeans and even Americans and English were guilty. For such crimes, "Let LIBERTY blush and CHRISTIANITY hide her dishonoured head," wrote Rowson.

In an effort to capture the interest of her female audience and because of her continuing interest in women, Rowson included in her geography book commentary on the position of women in various countries in the east, implying that most non-Christian and undemocratic countries did not treat women acceptably. In Turkey women "seldom or ever [went] abroad, or [were] seen by any but their nearest relations" (107). Egyptian women were not admitted to the society of men, not even at table, but [remained] standing, or seated in a corner of the room while the husband [dined]" (141). Tibetans "considered women as very inferior to men; that they were created only to people the world, and to look after the household affairs" (110). More positively, she praised the town of Oise in Beauvais:

[It was] remarkable for having been defended by the women, under the conduct of Joanne Hatchette, in 1463, when it was besieged by the duke of Burgundy. They obliged the duke to raise the siege; and in memory of their exploits, the women always walk first in the procession on the 10th of July, the anniversary of their deliverance. (101)

Later Rowson texts would explicitly define an acceptable role for women.

These passages indicate Rowson's own biases, as a conscientious textbook writer was expected to do. Most of the book is judiciously presented, and even in her most subjective moments she appeared no less objective than her contemporaries. Nathan Dwight's 1795 *Short System of Geography*, for example, claimed that the Irish had no distinct customs except "their funeral howlings and presenting their corpses in the streets to excite the charity of passers-by."[3] Rowson's style is straightforward, with concise and clear sentences that read easily. Though of necessity she took most of her information from printed sources, as all writers of geography books did, she also relied upon her own knowledge, and her selection of material as well as her style made the information highly readable.

The "Geographical Exercises" in this textbook reflect another of Rowson's great interests, navigation. Having a father and three half brothers who were seamen, Rowson had learned navigation early and enjoyed reading books on the subject. She considered it a worthwhile subject for young women, even for young girls. In *An Abridgment of Universal Geography* she attributed to navigation the chief advancements in the study of geography and then, in a series of questions, each building on the previous answer, instructed her pupils in rudimentary navigation principles. She taught first how to find the latitude and longitude of a place and then how to find a place once given the latitude and longitude. She taught means of measuring the distance from one place to another and the way to rectify the globe. Her definitions and explanations of esoteric terms (such as the ecliptic and the rational horizon) would be instructive to most present-day adults. Clearly Rowson's idea of the educated woman extended beyond knowledge of mending and doing accounts.

The "Historical Exercises" which follow the "Geographical Exercises" contain a brief but interesting account of the Revolutionary War. With a remarkable objectivity and a sympathy for both sides that one seldom finds in histories before the twentieth century, Rowson described the origins, development, and conclusion of the conflict. Her experiences as a bipartisan enabled her not only to understand why both countries felt as they did but also to explain those feelings succinctly and clearly to the next generation.

Rowson published this text with John West, a bibliographer and scholar who published most of her other texts as well. She could not expect a wide circulation for a schoolbook, but she could use the printed copies herself and make it available for other schools in the area with students from eleven to sixteen years old. The book had "some popularity in its day" and then appeared again in booksellers' catalogs between 1811 and 1815. No second edition, however, has been located.[4]

Youth's First Steps in Geography. In the next few years Rowson found herself adapting her geography text for younger pupils, and in 1818 she published *Youth's First Steps in Geography*. This book begins with a note to instructors, explaining how the text can be used most effectively. It follows a question-and-answer format, proceeding from the simple "What is Geography?" through questions detailing North American national and state boundaries and ending with difficult questions of navigation. Rowson believed that even her youngest pupils should learn elementary principles of navigation and know maps of their state, country, and the world, though she did reduce the quantity of material for younger girls. As in her first geography text, she combined facts, religious teachings, and moral judgments, but the greatest part of the book is objectively and compactly stated fact. Conspicuously absent are the moral fables and apologues that characterized her other writings, both novels and textbooks. The book contains no personal comments and suggests none of the personal prejudices that make the *Abridgment of Universal Geography* so interesting. The style is so straightforward and matter-of-fact that a modern reader marvels at the patience of children who memorized even part of the 178 pages. The book was published by the Boston firm of Wells and Lilly, the Boston outlet for the publications of Philadelphian Mathew Carey, with whom Rowson had done business in earlier years.

Spelling Dictionary. Rowson's *Spelling Dictionary* (1807), like the geography texts, was written to serve her own teaching needs. When she first began teaching, she explained in the preface, she discovered students who could "read"—pronounce the words and pause at appropriate punctuation marks—but who could not understand, because they did not know the meaning of the words. Since spelling books taught merely spelling, dictionaries offered only definitions (usually in forms beyond a child's comprehension), and grammar books defined parts of speech, none of these books alone could attack the problem. Rowson therefore combined these three into one spelling dictionary. The book consists of over four hundred lessons of twenty to twenty-five words each. Each word is spelled with syllabic separations, the part of speech abbreviated, and all etymologies omitted. A short definition, usually a synonymous word or phrase, is given for each entry.

Rowson's approach seems remarkably ahead of her time. She sought in her teaching not simply to make her students memorize but to be able to associate ideas and to think, so that they could continue their education independently. Children who were taught mechanically to read and pronounce, she said, were not educated "unless we teach them to associate ideas; and this cannot be done if they do not know the exact meaning of every word."[5] She wanted lessons to have meaning for the students, not to serve merely as classroom requirements. "Children study with more cheerfulness when the lesson is short and determined." "It is my fixed opinion," she insisted, "that it is better to give the young pupil one rational idea, than fatigue them by obliging them to commit to memory a thousand mere words" (iii).

Evidence of Rowson's exacting standards appears in the dictionary's level of difficulty. Many of the entries would challenge adolescents ("calamus," "expatiate," "obviate," "vilify") and some are simply out of the realm of their experience ("Baubee," "habeas corpus"). Others, however, are words the students might encounter in novels ("macaroni," "rack rent"), and many are simply ordinary and useful words ("monarchical," "olfactory," "wrench"). Many of the words are those students might encounter in their readings of history, the classics, or natural science, but some are drawn from the law.

At the end of the dictionary a reader finds four pages entitled "A Concise Account of the Heathen Deities, and Other Fabulous Persons; with the Heroes and Heroines of Antiquity." Rowson seems to have been familiar only with Latin deities, however, as no Greek entries appear.

The first edition of the *Spelling Dictionary* was published by John West, the publisher of *An Abridgment of Universal Geography*. The book circulated widely and was found in many booksellers' catalogs, necessitating a second edition in 1815, published in Portland, Maine.[6]

Exercises in History, Chronology, and Biography. One of Rowson's last writing efforts, produced intermittently between bouts of illness, was *Exercises in History, Chronology, and Biography in Question and Answer*, published by Richardson and Lord in 1822. With its long subtitle (see Bibliography), the book was published in 1822, at a time when few other textbooks of history existed. Although other history books had appeared on the market in the decades after the Revolution, few if any attempted to cover world history, so once again Rowson's effort was probably the first of its kind in the country.[7] By publishing this early history, she anticipated a wave of such textbooks which were to appear in the next few decades. She opened the book with a chatty preface, for, unlike the days when she had written her first fiction, fearful of critical reaction and intimidated by having to write a preface, she now felt confident of herself, her audience, and the reception her book would encounter. As with her geography and spelling books, she offered this work to other teachers in hopes they would find it useful.

Divided into thirteen "Exercises," the book takes the form of questions and answers, tracing the history of the world from the time of creation to the founding of the American republic, moving through histories of Greece, Rome, England, modern Europe, Russia, Turkey, the Middle East, and the United States, omitting parts of Asia and all of Africa, probably because Rowson lacked sources for these regions. Besides the conventional history of politics, which alone might seem tiresome to her students, Rowson's history includes art, literature, architecture, and invention as well as colorful personalities. The historical figures include many women, many of them generally unknown:

Q. What illustrious female lived about A.D. 1081?

A. Anna Commina, daughter to the emperor Alexius Commenus whose elegant writings gave celebrity to her father's reign. About this time the Turks invaded the eastern empire, and they finally conquered Asia Minor, A.D. 1084.[8]

Other women in history include Boadicia, Margaret of Denmark, notable for her "great qualities for government and policy," Queen Christina of Sweden for her support of learning, and Queen Anne of England for her illustrious reign. To find role models for her young women students, Rowson continued to read history throughout her life.

As in her other texts, her style here is clear and concise. Each question is answered succinctly in paragraph form, thus avoiding the tedium of lists of dates or chronicles of kings. The first questions define her terms ("What is History?" "What is Biography?" "What is Chronology?") and establish a reason for studying the subject. ("Of what use is the connexion [sic] of these studies?") Some questions permit a brief narration, such as the history of Elizabeth and Mary Queen of Scots, reminiscent of the stories Rowson used in her fiction.

For the modern reader Rowson's blending of biblical and secular history may appear disconcerting, but most nineteenth-century Americans believed the Bible was as factual as any other history book, and for Rowson to avoid the story of creation and the major incidents in the Old and New Testaments would have constituted a curious omission. In her writing of religious history Rowson was displaying the increased interest in religion she acquired in her later years and demonstrated in her last novels.

Rowson published this book with Richardson and Lord, at the time a two-year-old company destined to become one of the first United States firms to concentrate almost entirely on publication of textbooks.[9] The book enjoyed some popularity in its day, according to Rowson's bibliographer.[10]

Biblical Dialogues.   The interest Rowson displayed in religion in *Exercises in History* culminated in her last textbook. *Biblical Dialogues Between a Father and His Family*, also published by Richardson and Lord in 1822. This eight-hundred-page, two-volume work required in Rowson's last years a great deal of time and study, for it in effect retold all the main stories of the Old and New Testaments together with some ancient history and some history of the medieval church. To write it, Rowson read the biblical commentators Campe, Stackhouse, Poole, Prideaux, Calmet, Wells, and Shuckford. To appeal to young readers, she told the Bible stories within a narrative framework, somewhat similar to Enos Hitchcock's *Memoirs of the Bloomsgrove Family*. Reverend Alworth tells the stories to his children Horatio, Charilea, Amy, and the twins, James and John. Their dialogue keeps the stories moving swiftly. The characters are realistic, and even the biblical characters become believable human beings with everyday emotions, as the Alworth family compare their own motivations to those of Abraham, Esther, Judith, and so on.

As in her other texts, Rowson included stories about and of interest to other women. Queen Esther suffers the fear and trembling of a novel heroine when she approaches her king, but in the end receives her reward as "his equal, queen, and companion."[11] More important as models for her readers, Rowson's modern characters, the Alworth girls, question their father for reasonable explanations of events just as their brothers do. They do not sit back in mute acceptance, and their father seems to expect them to respond with their heads as well as their hearts. Rowson thus countered the prejudice against women's participation in religious matters and encouraged her students to speak up, as the Alworth girls do.

Both the biblical stories and the narrative framework include themes familiar to readers of Rowson: filial piety, humility, the rewards of virtue, and the rewards of suffering. The book also stresses her belief in a rational rather than emotional approach to religion. As she had made clear in the *Abridgment of Universal Geography*, she disliked a religion such as Catholicism that empowers one central figure and a hierarchy of priests to do all the thinking. Rowson insisted that her women think for themselves, relying neither on priest nor husband. When the children ask questions about the probability of biblical occurrences, Mr. Alworth replies with logical and scientific answers. The burning of the golden calf, he explains, probably took place by means of a process of "burning glass" recently discovered by the Royal Academy in Paris. He answers other questions with homey explanations, and he sometimes stresses the metaphorical nature of Scripture. Rowson's definition of religion may sound emotional ("a cheerful, contented disposition—a heart greateful [*sic*] for every blessing, and resigned to the all-wise dispensations of Providence. . . ." [2:105]), but she clearly did not intend emotion to overshadow reason.

Her belief in the depravity of human nature, echoed again and again in her novels, reappeared in *Biblical Dialogues*. "We are none of us without fault, we are all prone to evil from our very childhood" (1:36). In this respect Rowson sounded more seventeenth century than nineteenth, and indeed she did not share the sentimental love tradition of woman as the religious and moral superior. She believed in moral equality as well as intellectual equality.

A Present for Young Ladies. Perhaps the most significant of Rowson's texts is *A Present for Young Ladies* (1811), for it gives the reader a real sense of Rowson as educator. This book collects some of the essays, poems, and dialogues presented at her annual exhibitions, the first of which was held in Franklin Hall on Nassau Street, Boston, on October 14, 1802. Rowson's theatrical experience naturally led her to display her students' talents before an audience of parents and neighbors who would relish the opportunity to see their daughters shine and who might witness the care Rowson exercised in educating young women as their parents wished. By the time she published *A Present for Young Ladies*, the exhibitions had become so popular that they drew an audience not only of parents and friends but of interested citizens willing to pay the fifty-cent admission charge.[12] Rowson wrote all the pieces for these exhibitions, and her students recited them. The works range from short poems for very young students, such as "The Bee," (delivered "by a little miss nine years old") to full-length addresses read by the oldest pupils; and they include dialogues for two and three participants, a condensed "Outline of Universal History," a brief "Rise and Progress of Navigation," and the popular "Sketches of Biography." The most striking image conveyed in all of these pieces is of the educated, independent woman. The book characterizes Rowson's school as an unconventional academy where women learn self-respect and the importance of education.

Many of the selections emphasize the need for and kind of education young women should have. While she admitted a woman's first obligations are to her domestic duties, Rowson did not dwell on these. "When literature, or the study of fine arts, can be engaged in, without neglect of our feminine duties, why may we not attain the goal of perfection as well as the other sex?"[13] Rowson concentrated on the education a woman needs after she has acquired her domestic skills. Education is a woman's most important right. "The mind of a female is certainly as capable of acquiring knowledge as that of the other sex" (151). Although women need not "study with that closeness of application which is essentially requisite in the education of a boy" (153), women should do more than dabble at intellectual subjects, and they should not disguise their education:

Many are the prejudices entertained, and the witticisms thrown out against what are called learned women; but surely a woman will not be less acceptable in the world, or worse qualified for performing her part in it, for having devoted a large portion of her early years to the cultivation of her understanding. (151)

How is a woman to manage reading and studying "huge volumes" of history and five-or six-hundred page poems? By "order, regularity, and habitual industry," exactly as Rowson had educated herself while fulfilling her domestic, social, and career responsibilities.

Rowson looked to history to teach contemporary women how to live. Her essay, the "Outline of Universal History," presents figures who instruct by means of example—some to follow, some to avoid. The essay on "The Rise and Progress of Navigation" concisely summarizes the history of navigation, a subject Rowson believed necessary because it "extend[s] the geographical knowledge of mankind, and facilitate[s] that commercial intercourse, which is a fountain of wealth to every nation where it is encouraged." Unlike those who argued against increased commerce as a discouragement to American manufacture, Rowson believed commerce would stimulate the American economy as well as its arts.[14]

But the historical lessons both students and exhibition audiences found most exciting were the "Sketches of Female Biography." Rowson combed through biblical and secular history, both ancient and modern, to find "innumerable instances of female courage, fortitude, talent and virtue of every description" (84). "It would be absurd," she argued, "to imagine that talents or virtue were confined to sex or station" (84). To prove that women need not be "the weaker sex," she presented biographies of Chelonis, daughter of a king of Sparta, who accompanied her husband in his exile, and Eponia, a Roman woman who lived in a subterranean vault for nine years to help her husband evade his enemies. Women can, insisted Rowson, prove "themselves adequate to every trial, that proves their attachment to their husbands, children, parents or country" (90). To disprove the notion that women cannot keep secrets, she told of Tymicho of Lacedemonia and Leona of Athens, both of whom feared talking under enemy torture and so bit off their own tongues (97). To show the heights of learning that women can attain she provided several examples of women who mastered languages and "the most abstruse sciences." She also included women who faced death in battle and women heads of state, Queen Elizabeth of England and Catherine of Russia. From modern history she included such women as Catherine Cline, the actress, and the historian Catherine Macaulay.

The dialogues were another popular part of the program at the exhibitions. Performed by groups of two or three students, these dialogues derived from Rowson's theatrical experience. They invited pantomime, and their success depended on the degree of the students'

stage talents. Combining humor with didacticism, the dialogues sati-
rize sentimental novels and the vanity of fashion, and emphasize the
students' need for assiduous study. Rowson effected humor from the
four-beat couplets and the colloquial language:

> I abominate reading, it makes one so dumpish
> And as to our governess, la! she's so frumpish,
> 'Miss, do mind your work, do child sit upright.
> Miss, your frock is unpin'd, dear how badly you write.
>
> (22)

One dialogue even deals with politics, as one character sternly lectures
another on the need for increased commerce and the necessity for going to war with Britain and standing up against Napoleon. Rowson
used Napoleon as an example of a tyrant:

> He stole regal ermine, and stain'd it with blood;
> Oh, Mary, remember how Louis has died,
> That Louis who fought on America's side.
>
> (34)

She reduced Napoleon's tyranny to the domestic level, describing him
as a cruel husband:

> [He] beats and locks up his wife . . .
> I warrant she's oftentimes pinched black and blue.
> Her chains tho' of gold, she may keep for all me,
> I'm content to be poor, tho I may but be free.
>
> (31)

Tyranny was unacceptable to Rowson in either government or marriage.

Perhaps the most interesting aspect of this book is that Rowson
wrote it for public presentation by women at a time when Americans
suffered from prejudice against women speaking in public. Only
Quakers permitted women to address a church, and women who
dared speak before an audience sometimes felt obliged to apologize for
their audacity. The speaker of the 1794 Philadelphia Ladies' Academy
commencement address, for example, made this apology:

Were I voluntarily to offer myself a candidate for the purpose of addressing
so respectable an audience, through any other motive than that of complying

with the rules of the institution, I should consider the most elaborate apology, insufficient to extenuate such a violation of female delicacy.[15]

Rowson, however, offered no apologies.

Poetry

These textbooks were not the author's only creative outlet during these years. In 1804, her first year at Newton, Rowson collected and published *Miscellaneous Poems*. This was her second and last collection of poetry, as her first collection of verse, *Poems on Various Subjects*, had appeared in London in 1789. No known copies of that early work exist today. When *Miscellaneous Poems* appeared, Rowson's reputation was so extensive that she published the book by subscription and compiled an impressive list of 245 names, including leading Medford, Newton, and Boston families.

The poems show Rowson as a poet of moderate abilities whose form and subject matter vary widely. The poems range from short occasional pieces to lengthy patriotic works, with great variation in rhyme scheme and length of lines. Some of the verses are actually songs, elsewhere set to music; some are "sonnets," a term Rowson used loosely to refer to short poems in a variety of meters. A ballad entitled "Maria, Not a Fiction" relates a plot similar to that of *Charlotte Temple*, and in fact includes lines found on the title page of that novel.

Some of the most popular verse in early nineteenth-century America reflected an intense nationalism, such as Joel Barlow's *Columbiad*, and the best of the poems in this Rowson collection are the patriotic verses, written to commemorate particular events. By 1804, Rowson had earned a reputation as a writer of occasional pieces, one of her first having been "The Standard of Liberty," a poetical address to the United States Army performed in Baltimore in 1795 by Eliza Whitlock.[16] This work was included in *Miscellaneous Poems* and traces the standard of liberty from Greece to Rome and thence to Columbia, a favorite theme in post-Revolutionary American poetry. The poem ends:

> The music ceas'd, the Standard glorious rose
> A youthful hand the heavenly pledge enclose
> To guard it, & repel invading foes;
> When LIBERTY in robes transcendent bright,
> Her head encircled with a crown of light

> Thus with a smile the warlike legion owns,
> "Columbia is my home, Her Warriors are my sons."[17]

The Baltimore audience had responded enthusiastically to this tribute, especially when delivered by a favorite actress, and Rowson had,
on the basis of this success, been invited in Boston to write a piece
for the celebration of Washington's birthday. *Miscellaneous Poems* also
contains a eulogy on the death of Washington, which suggests the
conservative tone that pervades many of these occasional poems.
Washington warns against dangers of change and faction:

> "My friends, my fellow-citizens, said He,
> "Be still unanimous, be great and free;
> "For know, a state may soon be rendered weak
> "By foreign faction or by private pique;
> "Let not corruption e'er your judgment blind;
> "Preserve with care an independent mind;
> "Support, revere the laws; believe me, friends,
> "Your all on unanimity depends.
> "By faction, all would be to chaos hurl'd;
> "Be but united, and defy the world."
>   (53–54)

This same conservatism extends not only through poems occasioned
by political events and figures but through other poems as well.
When comparing the more radical ideas contained in Rowson's novels
with the staid traditionalism of the poems, a reader is reminded that
poetry during the eighteenth century was regarded as the more serious, noble, and uplifting genre. Perhaps too Rowson's subscription
list of proper Bostonians inclined her toward traditional views.

One particularly interesting poem displays a traditional view of
woman and therefore an inconsistency in Rowson's thought. The
"Rights of Woman," presented first by a young Miss Warner at an
annual exhibition of the Medford academy, enthusiastically extols domestic bliss. The poem so blatantly contradicts much of Rowson's life
and thought that it may have been written to reassure her audience
of parents that their daughters would not become radicalized under
her tutelage. It appears as the product of a conservative period in her
life, when she sought to suppress her feminism in favor of a traditional image appealing to the upwardly mobile middle class of Medford. The poem stresses domesticity, defining women's rights in
terms of their obligations to men; their rights to be competent in the

household, to make "a paradise at home," and to share the woes of male members of the family.

The conservatism in this poem, however, is qualified by the poem that follows it. In "Women as They Are" all women's faults are attributed to men and to a culture that educates women inadequately. The poem satirizes various ways of raising girls, especially the practice of teaching little girls that they are love objects:

> Ere one proper wish her heart can move,
> She's taught to think of lovers, and of love;
> She's told she is a beauty, does not doubt it;
> What need of sense? beauties can wed without it.
> And then her eyes, her teeth, her lips, her hair,
> And shape, are all that can be worth her care;
> She thinks a kneeling world should bow before her,
> and men were but created to adore her.
>
> (108)

The poem also ridicules a woman with no interest outside her home:

> [A woman] whose only merit lies
> In making puddings, good preserves, and pies;
> Who rises with Aurora, blyth and cheery,
> Feeds pigs and poultry, overlooks her dairy. . .
> What is there else that's worth a woman's larnings? [sic]
> With my good will, a girl should never look
> In any but a pray'r or cook'ry book:
> Reading 'bout kings, and states, and foreign nations,
> Will only fill their heads with proclamations.
>
> (108)

The contrast between "Rights of Woman" and "Women as They Are" may be a tribute to the adaptability Rowson demonstrated so often throughout her life.

Her translation of Horatian odes in this collection of poems is the only known evidence of her knowledge of Latin, probably acquired during her days as a governess in England.[18] Even in these translations Rowson selects odes with themes congenial to her own values, the eighteenth ode from the Second Book of Horace, for example, extolling the virtues of the "middle sphere" of life.

The variety of form and subject in *Miscellaneous Poems* suggests that Rowson enjoyed toying with poetry. She has short poems, long poems, formal odes, and rhythmic ballads. All of the poems are rhymed, but rhyme schemes vary widely, from couplets to twelve-line stanzas. In keeping with the variety of subject matter popular in other poetry of the day, Rowson's subjects range from nature and immortality to patriotism, including the ethereal, abstract, and concrete. The book apparently enjoyed some popularity, at least in Boston. In addition to its subscribers, *Miscellaneous Poems* was also sold by the printers Gilbert & Dean and by booksellers W. P. and L. Blake.[19] In November, 1804, the *Monthly Anthology* reviewed it, expressing appreciation of the sentiments and intentions of the poems but not Rowson's poetic abilities.[20] Some forty years later the influential Evert and George Duyckinck anthologized some of the verses and praised the poems as "expressive of [a] generous woman's heart."[21]

Journalism

Another of Rowson's literary activities during her life as an educator was journalism. While teaching and administering her school at Medford, she began to contribute to various local journals and magazines, in keeping with her new position as Boston academic and literateur. The first decade of the nineteenth century witnessed a great surge of magazines in Boston, many of them religious, some exclusively literary, and many, like the *Boston Weekly Magazine* with which Rowson became associated, miscellanies.[22] The *Boston Weekly Magazine*, published by Gilbert and Dean between October 30, 1802, and October 19, 1805, advertised that it devoted its pages to "morality, literature, biography, history, the fine arts, agriculture, etc."

Although Rowson's early biographers, Knapp, Nason, and Vail, assumed Rowson actually edited this periodical, evidence suggests otherwise. First, it seems unlikely that Rowson would have undertaken an unrewarding job at a time when she was fully and profitably occupied. Magazine editing had little to commend it at this time, for it involved financing, establishing the distribution, and marshalling sufficient contributors or else doing most of the writing onself. "Benjamin Bickerstaff, Esquire," writing in the Baltimore *Observer* during the first decade of the century, described an editor's difficulties:

The occupation of an editor is one in which unremitted corporeal labour earns but a small and precarious recompense; and much literary taste must be exerted with a very humble portion of the meed of fame.[23]

As a result, some magazines engaged multiple editors and others were edited by their publishers.

Second, textual evidence indicates the the *Boston Weekly Magazine* was edited not by Rowson but by the publishers, Gilbert and Dean. In volume 2 on October 19, 1805, p. 205, the concluding issue, they wrote, "This Number concludes the third volume of the *Boston Weekly Magazine*; and with it the present publishers conclude their editorial labours." The publishers of the *Boston Magazine*, to whom Gilbert and Dean bequeathed their publication, wrote in the first issue that they had made arrangements with the "late editors" of the *Boston Weekly Magazine*. Further, the editors spoke of Rowson's novel *Sincerity* as though it had been submitted like any other manuscript.[24] A year after the serialized chapters of this Rowson novel had begun, the publishers reported a fire in their printing office, but noted that the latest installments had been saved because the manuscript happened to be "in the apartments of the Editors."[25]

Of course, Rowson assisted Gilbert and Dean in at least one of their editorial capacities by writing many articles, and the idea that she edited the magazine may have arisen from what were assumed to be her substantial contributions. Although few articles have even identifying initials, Nason's contention that Rowson wrote the "Gossip" columns seems inconclusive.[26] On the one hand, the essays in this column covered such subjects as the education of young women, dress, filial piety, raising an adopted daughter, false female friendships, and other moral topics that recall much of Rowson's fiction. The columns occasionally included letters from readers voicing interruptions similar to those in *Charlotte Temple*: " 'Dear me, Mr. Gossip' cries one of my fair readers. 'I declare if I am not out of all manner of patience. . . .' "[27] If the columns were not written by Rowson, they were the work of someone equally forthright: "Man has no more right to sin with impunity than woman," the writer declared.[28] "And why is not Chastity as necessary a virtue in man, as in woman?"[29] This defense of women also sounds like Rowson:

Slander is a vice with which the female sex have been charged, as practicing it in a more eminent degree than men; . . . But where interest in any mercantile pursuit or indeed where competition exists even in arts, sciences, or literature men are often as guilty of it, in as criminal a degree as women.[30]

This point is made in each of Rowson's novels.

On the other hand, one column sounds quite unlike Susanna Rowson, and that is the one on the subject of church music, a topic of widespread controversy even as late as 1803.[31] Singing schools had grown up in the eighteenth century as an indigenous American institution, but they still carried a slightly lower-class connotation and sometimes were criticized for bringing young women and men together in too romantic or suggestive an atmosphere. Choirs grew out of singing schools, and many New England church congregations divided over whether to permit the local singing school to establish a choir for church services. The Medford town meeting had voted to establish a singing school in 1801, and in March, 1803, the town had established a choir in the First Church. By June the gossip columnist wrote that she did not like choirs or the singing of "newfangled tunes," a term widely used to refer to shape-note tunes or to hymns by Isaac Watts. As a singer and songwriter herself, Rowson would more likely have taken the opposite stand, in favor of improved church music by a choir who knew and appreciated music.

One other column suggests the Gossip was someone other than Rowson. In January, 1803, the columnist turned to the subject of novels. She recommended only three English novelists, "Miss Burney, Miss Lee, or Mrs. Brooke," all of whom Rowson had mentioned favorably in her novels. But among Americans the writer could recommend only Susanna Rowson, with qualifications:

even Rowson's works are not without dangerous tendency, and perhaps of all her numerous productions there are not more than three which could by an impartial Censor by recommended. Reuben and Rachel, an historical romance is the best, Charlotte and the Inquisitor, have a considerable degree of merit.[32]

Was this Rowson writing on Rowson? Very likely occasional Gossip columns were written by another hand.

When the *Boston Weekly Magazine* changed hands and became the *Boston Magazine*, Rowson contributed to the successor with less regularity. Gilbert and Dean sold their magazine to Joshua Belcher and Samuel T. Armstrong, who continued to issue the magazine weekly with the same material and format from October, 1805 to April, 1806. In May they changed the title to the *Emerald*, increased the number of pages, and reduced the page size, but after this time Rowson had no known connection with the magazine.[33]

Another magazine to which she contributed from 1806 to 1811 was the *Monthly Anthology, or Magazine of Polite Literature*.[34] When this magazine turned from reprinting English periodical literature to publishing a miscellany of American works, Rowson submitted pieces to it, but as none of them was signed or initialed, identification of her articles is difficult.

The only other periodical to which Rowson is known to have contributed is the *New England Galaxy*, a weekly established by Joseph Buckingham in 1817 when Rowson was fifty-five years old. For this magazine she wrote primarily religious verses, such as "The Wedding Supper" (a poem based on Matthew 22, printed May 15, 1818), and "The Mighty Lord" (printed June 19, 1818). Joseph Buckingham wrote warmly and with admiration of Susanna Rowson in his *Personal Memoirs*.[35]

Chapter Six

Conclusion

Rowson's contributions to American literature are greater than the sum of her publications. Those publications reflect an impressive versatility, wide-ranging interests, and a love of various art forms, and as works of literature many of them deserve a modern edition. Rowson's literary accomplishments range not only among the standard forms: novels, plays, poetry, and essays; but she made significant contributions also among less frequently explored genres: song lyrics, librettos, translations, textbooks, and religious writings. America's first woman of letters thus offered her talents to a variety of types of American literature. But as important as those literary talents is her historical significance as an immigrant artist in the period of the new republic.

Rowson's biography parallels the thought of the age in which she lived. From her childhood in Nantasket, Massachusetts, she imbibed ideas from both the patriot James Otis and her Tory father and came to love New England and New Englanders. From her youth in London she absorbed the traditions of the popular stage and the eighteenth-century woman's novel, learning from Thomas Harris of Covent Garden and William Lane of the Minerva Press the stilted and conventional prose style and conventional morality that appealed to popular taste. By the time she immigrated permanently to America, she could adapt quickly to the American literary and theatrical public, learning from theatrical managers Wignell and Williamson as well as the influential publisher Mathew Carey. Like the new nation, Rowson showed herself to be eager, energetic, didactic, experimental, uncertain, opportunistic, and flexible. Her literary battle with William Cobbett politicized her and made her more conservative. Then, like the maturing nation, Rowson settled down in the nineteenth century to become a proper Bostonian, again picking up on a current trend by dedicating her life to women's education.

As a writer Rowson deserves attention for both reflecting current taste in style and morality and at the same time criticizing it. Some of her heroines may be categorized as stereotypical of sentimental novels and others introduce new types of women characters, independent-minded adventurers. Rowson both follows the standard seduction-novel plots and departs from them. Most notably, her interest in women—as historical figures, as subjects for fiction, and as thinking citizens in a democratic nation—distinguishes her among writers of the eighteenth century and attracts readers today.

Notes and References

Preface

1. R. W. G. Vail, *Susanna Haswell Rowson, the Author of Charlotte Temple. A Bibliographical Study* (Worcester, 1933), 27.
2. Review of *Charlotte's Daughter, American Ladies' Magazine*, April 1829, 190–91.
3. Evert and George Duyckinck, *Cyclopedia of American Literature* (New York: Scribner, 1855) 1:502–4.
4. Thomas Wentworth Higginson and Henry Wolcott Boynton, *A Reader's History of American Literature* (Boston: Houghton Mifflin, 1904), 92–93.
5. W. P. Trent and John Erskine, *Great American Writers* (New York: Henry Holt, 1912), 12.
6. Carl Van Doren, *The American Novel* (New York: Macmillan, 1912), 7–8.
7. Henry B. Dawson, *New York City During the American Revolution* (New York: Mercantile Library Association, 1861), iv.
8. *Charlotte Temple* (New York: Funk & Wagnalls, 1905).
9. Frederick Lewis Pattee, *The First Century of American Literature* (New York: Appleton-Century, 1935), 86–90.
10. Arthur Hobson Quinn, *American Fiction: An Historical and Critical Survey* (New York: Appleton-Century, 1936), 192.
11. Vail, *Bibliographical Study.*
12. Ed. Clara M. and Rudolph Kirk *Charlotte Temple* (New Haven: College and University Press, 1964).
13. One dissertation has been published on Rowson: Dorothy Weil, *In Defense of Women* (University Park: Pennsylvania State University Press, 1976).

Chapter One

1. The Baptismal Register of the Parish of St. Thomas cites a baptismal date, but the date of Rowson's birth is not known.
2. John Spargo's biography of Anthony Haswell (Rutland: Tuttle, 1925) claims that Susanna Musgrave was the daughter of William Musgrave, Commissioner of Customs. This claim, however, appears unfounded. Sir William Musgrave (1735–1800), born in Cumberland, married Lady Carlyle and died without issue, according to a letter from T. G. Smith, HMS Cus-

toms and Excise, London. However, William Playfair's *British Baronetage* (London: Reynolds and Grace, 1811), 6:52, states that Sir William Musgrave is an incorrect identification of Sir Philip Musgrave, who married Jane Turton and fathered nine children. None of his daughters was named Susanna.

3. *Portsmouth Rate Book*, cited in a letter from Miss R. Phillips, Portsmouth Record Office, August 6, 1980.

4. G. D. Scull, ed., "The Montresor Journals," *The New-York Historical Society Quarterly* 14 (1881):4–5.

5. Portsmouth Marriage, Baptismal and Burial Registers, cited in letters from R. Phillips, Portsmouth Record Office, September 4 and August 6, 1980.

6. H. Sargeant, "A History of Portsmouth Theatres," *Portsmouth Papers* 13 (1971):3–11.

7. See *A List of the Polls and of the Estates, Real and Personal* (Hull, Mass. 1775), 66, 133, Boston State House.

8. *Rebecca; or, The Fille de Chambre* (Philadelphia: H. & T. Rice, 1794), 161; hereafter page references cited in parentheses in the text.

9. William Sweetser, *King's Handbook of Boston Harbor* (Boston: Moses King Corp., 1888), 40. After a nineteenth-century remodeling, the house was purchased by the poet John Boyle O'Reilly (d. 1890) and stands today as the Hull Public Library. Today the house looks much as it did when O'Reilly lived in it.

10. F. W. Howay, "A Short Account of Robert Haswell," *Washington Historical Quarterly* 24 (1933):83–90.

11. Sweetser, *Boston Harbor*, 38. The young Haswell may also have had access to a circulating library in Nantasket.

12. Samuel Lorenzo Knapp, "A Memoir of the Author," in *Charlotte's Daughter; or, the Three Orphans* (Boston, 1828), 5.

13. See Solomon Lincoln, *History of the Town of Hingham, Plymouth Country, Mass.* (Hingham: Caleb, Farnum & Brown, 1827) for an account of the town during the Revolution.

14. See his letters in the Barrett Collection, University of Virginia.

15. For a description of the battle, see W. M. James, *The British Navy in Adversity: A Study of the War of American Independence* (1926; reprint, New York: Russell & Russell, 1970), 38.

16. The incident is recounted in *Rebecca; or, the Fille de Chambre.*

17. For an account of the experiences common to loyalists like Haswell, see Mary Beth Norton, *The British-Americans: The Loyalist Exiles in England, 1774–1789* (London, 1974), 25–26.

18. *Massachusetts Archives*, 211:94,87.

19. Peter Force, *American Archives*, 4th ser. (Washington: M. St. Claire Clarke and Peter Force, 1834), 4:1282.

20. William Haswell recalled these men gratefully years later in En-

gland, and Susanna Rowson thanked them publicly in the preface to *Trials of the Human Heart.*

21. *Massachusetts Archives*, 88:441.

22. Edward Alfred Jones, *The Loyalists of Massachusetts*, (1930; reprint, Baltimore, 1969), 161.

23. Haswell recounts some of her experiences as a governess in *Rebecca; or, the Fille de Chambre*, in passages she attested were autobiographical.

24. Haswell wrote at least one song for Vauxhall, the public pleasure gardens south of the Thames in London. A copy of her "Willy of the Dale" sung by "Miss Milne" is in the possession of the Houghton Library, Harvard University, Cambridge, Mass. It bears no date of publication and is not listed in Vail.

25. Jones, *Loyalists*, 161–62.

26. Philip Highfill reports that he has found a Rowson who provided "hardware" for the London Covent Garden theater, and this merchant may have been William Rowson's father. For information about the acting careers of both Susanna and William Rowson, I am indebted to Philip Highfill who sent me a typescript of his unpublished entries for the *Biographical Dictionary of Actors, Actresses, Musicians, Dancers, Managers & Other Stage Personnel in London 1600–1800* (Carbondale: Southern Illinois University Press, 1975-).

27. *Sarah; or, The Exemplary Wife* (Boston, 1813), 4.

28. Rowson was quoting from John Gregory's *A Father's Legacy to His Daughters* (Portsmouth, N.H.: Melcher & Osborne, 1786), 140.

29. See Vera Mobray Roberts, *On Stage: A History of Theatre* (New York: Harper & Row, 1962).

30. See Charles B. Hogan, *The London Stage, 1778–1800. A Critical Introduction* (Carbondale, 1968), lxvii–lxxii.

31. Roberts, *On Stage*, 266.

32. William B. Wood, *Personal Recollections of the Stage* (Philadelphia: William C. Baird, 1855), 92.

33. Thomas Clark Pollock, *The Philadelphia Theatre in the Eighteenth Century* (Philadelphia: University of Pennsylvania Press, 1933), 60.

34. Robert Haswell to Susanna Rowson, January 20, 1796 and May 19, 1796, Barrett Collection, University of Virginia.

35. William Clapp, *A Record of the Boston Stage* (1853; reprint, St. Clair Shores, 1970), 19–40.

36. See John Alden, "A Season in Federal Street. J. B. Williamson and the Boston Theatre, 1796–97," Proceedings of the American Antiquarian Society 65 (April, 1956):29–30, and the Allen A. Brown Collection on the Federal Street Theatre, Boston Public Library, for details about the Boston company.

37. Knapp, "Memoir," 9–10.

38. Mary Batchelder to Elias Nason, September 11, 1861, Barrett Collection, University of Virginia.

39. See Charles Brooks, *History of Medford: 1630–1855* (Boston, 1855), 298–99.

40. An unidentified newspaper clipping in the Barrett Collection comments on William Rowson's drinking and poor work at the Customs House.

41. See Moses Foster Sweetser, *King's Handbook of Newton, Massachusetts* (Boston: Moses King, 1889), 44–46.

42. F. W. Howay, "A Short Account of Robert Haswell," *Washington Historical Quarterly* 24 (1933):89–90.

43. See the ad in the *Columbia Centinel*, April 15, 1807. Another resident of the Newton household, according to S. F. Smith, *History of Newton, Mass., Town & City* (Boston: American Logotype Co., 1880), 107, was "one son," apparently the illegitimate child of William whom Susanna was said to have taken in and raised.

44. Walter Kendall Watkins, "The Great Street to Roxbury Gate: 1730–1830," *Bostonian Society Publications*, 2d ser., 3 (1919):89–126.

45. Charles C. Perkins and John S. Dwight, *From the Foundation of the Society through its Seventy-Fifth Season*, in *The History of the Handel and Haydn Society* (Boston: Alfred Mudge & Son, 1883), 1:33–34.

46. *Public Document Book* #235, 4, Boston Probate Court.

47. Elias Nason, *A Memoir of Mrs. Susanna Rowson* (Albany, 1870), 190.

48. Ibid., 159.

49. Knapp, "Memoir," 11.

50. Despite the evidence that the marriage was unsuccessful, Susanna Rowson wrote a love poem to her husband on their twenty-fifth wedding anniversary.

51. William Rowson wrote to his "hon. Parents" from Lisbon in 1811. An unsigned manuscript note in Nason's handwriting (Barrett Collection, University of Virginia) says that the young man died after 1820.

52. *Public Documents Book* #327, 44, Boston Probate Court.

53. One illegibly signed note in Nason's papers in the Barrett Collection claims that Susanna Rowson left seven or eight thousand dollars which fell into the hands of an adopted son. No evidence seems to exist for that claim.

54. *Deaths Registered in the City of Boston, 1801–1848*, Registry Division, Boston City Hall.

55. *Register of Marriages in Boston, 1800–1849*, Registry Division, Boston City Hall.

Chapter Two

1. Dorothy Blakey, *The Minerva Press, 1790–1820* (London, 1939), 48–49.

2. J. M. S. Tompkins, *The Popular Novel in England 1770–1800* (London, 1933), 9–10.

3. Ibid., 80–85.

4. This dedication may have led early biographers to conclude that Haswell served as governess to the duchess's children, but that claim appears unfounded. It is likely that Haswell was introduced to the duchess through her father's friends or perhaps her cousin, John Montresor, a man of wealth and influence.

5. Fanny Burney's Mrs. Tyrold is an example of a wife who carries her wedding vow of obedience beyond all reasonable expectation. See Tompkins, *Popular Novel,* 98, for discussion of this cult of submission.

6. *Victoria* (London, 1786), 1:77; hereafter volume and page references cited in parentheses in the text.

7. *Critical Review* (January, 1787), 76–77.

8. *Monthly Review* (January, 1787), 83.

9. Vail, *Bibliographical Study,* 31.

10. *The Inquisitor* (Philadelphia: Mathew Carey, 1794), 3:173–74.

11. Anon., "Review of *The Inquisitor,*" *Critical Review,* June, 1788, 568–69 (Appendix); Anon., "Review of *The Inquisitor,*" *Monthly Review,* August, 1788, 171.

12. Knapp, "Memoir," 11.

13. *Mary; or, The Test of Honour* (London: John Abraham, 1789), Preface; hereafter volume and page references cited in parentheses in the text.

14. Helena Wells, *Thoughts and Remarks on Establishing an Institution for the Support and Education of Unportioned Respectable Females* (London: Longman, Hurst, Rees, & Orne, 1809).

15. *Critical Review* (November, 1789) 408.

16. *Monthly Review* (March, 1790), 330.

17. The ongoing price for a manuscript was £5 to £25. See Tompkins, *Popular Novel,* 9–10.

18. *Mentoria,* 1; hereafter page references cited in parentheses in the text. Quotations are from the Dublin edition, published by Thomas Morton Bates for P. Wogan, A. Grueber, J. Halpern, J. Moore, R. M'Allister, J. Rice, J. Jones, and R. White, 1791.

19. See Mary Benson's *Women in the Eighteenth Century: A Study of Opinion and Social Usage* (New York: Columbia University Press, 1935) for a thorough discussion of the way middle-class men sent their daughters to schools to acquire the accomplishments of the upper classes, with the result that women moved out of the kitchen and into the parlor, considering themselves too good to do household labor.

20. Nason writes that "Urganda and Fatima" and one of the stories from the letters were included as models of fine writing in *The Young Ladies' Guide,* published by Thomas Andrews in 1799. Nason, *Memoir,* 41.

21. A. S. Collins, *The Profession of Letters* (New York, 1929), 44.

22. Ibid., 44, 113.

23. Blakey, *Minerva Press*, n.p.

24. See Frank Mumby, *Publishing and Bookselling: A History from the Earliest Times to the Present Day*, rev. ed. (London: Jonathan Cape, 1956), 178.

25. Vail, *Bibliographical Study*, 32.

26. *Critical Review*, 2d ser. (April, 1791), 468–69.

27. Vail, *Bibliographical Study*, 57.

28. "The Montresor Journals," ed. G. D. Scull, *New-York Historical Society Collections* 14 (1881):4.

29. *DNB* (1909), s.v. "John Burgoyne."

30. Lillie Deming Loshe, *The Early American Novel* (New York, 1907), 12.

31. *Charlotte: A Tale of Truth* (New Haven: College and University Press, 1964), 63; hereafter page references cited in parentheses in the text.

32. *Critical Review*, 2d ser., 1 (April, 1791): 68–69.

33. *Rebecca; or, the Fille de Chambre* (Philadelphia: H. & P. Rice and J. Rice & Co., 1794), v; hereafter page references cited in parentheses in the text.

34. Rowson changed the preface in the 1814 edition, and the changes are discussed below.

35. In the preface to the 1814 edition, Rowson verified the descriptions as autobiographical.

36. It would not have been unusual for a lord to seduce his children's governess in a day when marriage was often made for reasons other than love. In truth the eighteenth-century seduction novel warned readers against realistic dangers in a society that prized women's virginity while pregnancy was difficult to avoid.

37. Susanna Rowson to Anthony Haswell, May 21, 1795, Barrett Collection, University of Virginia.

Chapter Three

1. *A Trip to Parnassus* (London, 1788); hereafter page references cited in parentheses in the text.

2. See W. P. Courtney, "Edward Topham," *DNB* (1909). The asterisk referred to Rowson's footnote identifying Topham by name.

3. *DNB* (1909), s.v. "George Colman."

4. Tompkins, *The Popular Novel in England*, 125.

5. Quoted in Karl Mantzius, *History of Theatrical Art in Ancient and Modern Times*, trans. Louise von Cossel (1909: reprint, Gloucester: Peter Smith, 1979), 5:368.

6. See Roger Manvell's *Sarah Siddons: Portrait of an Actress* (New York: Putnam, 1971).

7. *The Thespian Dictionary, or Dramatic Biography of the Eighteenth Century* (London: J. Cundee, 1805), n.p.

8. *The World* was a newspaper run by Edward Topham, the playwright and journalist with whom Wells had been living for several years.

9. *Poems on Various Subjects* (London, 1788). No known copy exists.

10. *Monthly Review* (March, 1788), 241.

11. *Critical Review* (March, 1788), 225.

12. Another dramatist's work on the same topic as Rowson's *Slaves in Algiers* shows that interest in the subject remained high for several years after her play. *Slaves in Barbary* by Caleb Bingham dealt with a slave auction in Tunis, with the dialogue a debate between a slaver and the more humanitarian Bashaw of Tunis. This play was never performed but was published in *The Columbian Orator* in 1797. For a discussion of the play, see Walter J. Meserve, *An Emerging Entertainment: The Drama of the American People to 1828* (Bloomington, 1977), 156.

13. Charles Evans, *American Bibliography* (Chicago: Blakely Press, 1925) lists a second printing in 1796 but no known copies exist. Mathew Carey intended to include the play in a 1796 collection of American drama, but it is not known whether that intention ever materialized. See Roger Stoddard, "Some Corrigenda and addenda to Hill's American Plays Printed 1714–1830," *Papers of the Bibliographical Society of America* 65 (1971):278–95.

14. *Slaves in Algiers* (Philadelphia, 1794) 1.1.2; hereafter references to act, scene, and line cited in the text.

15. The most popular play of the period was John Daly Burke's *Bunker Hill; or the Death of General Warren*, which first appeared at the Boston Haymarket on February 17, 1797. Despite its flat characters, pompous blank verse, disjointed plot, and propagandistic speeches, the play enjoyed tremendous success, in part because audiences loved its spectacle. The production required construction of an actual hill which eighteen or twenty British could roll down when fired upon. It ended with a "Grand Procession in honor of General Warren," with "American music only" played between acts. See Meserve, *Emerging Entertainment*, 119–23.

16. George O. Seilhamer, *History of the American Theatre from 1774–1797* (New York: Harper, 1896), 3:182.

17. The *Baltimore Telegraph* of November 26, 1795, advertised it on the same program as *A Bold Stroke for a Husband* by Hannah Cowley.

18. Wignell's company was composed entirely of new English immigrants with the exception of one couple, Mr. and Mrs. Morris, and himself. Meserve (*Emerging Entertainment*, 127–28) concludes that theater

Meserve (*Emerging Entertainment*, 127–28) concludes that theater managers, themselves usually British, discriminated against American playwrights.

19. Meserve (*Emerging Entertainment*, 127–62) discusses plays and playwrights of this period.

20. Judith Sargent Murray wrote anonymous plays but refused to sign her name or even acknowledge them as her own.

21. "Calm Observer," *Daily Advertiser*, March 7, 1794, quoted in Meserve, *Emerging Entertainment*, 140.

22. William Cobbett, *A Kick for a Bite; or a Review Upon a Review; with a Critical Essay on the Works of Mrs. Rowson: in a letter to the editors of the American Monthly Review* (Philadelphia: Thomas Bradford, 1795), 78.

23. Ibid., 90.

24. Page Smith, *John Adams* (Garden City: Doubleday, 1956), 956.

25. *The Complete Works of Nathaniel Hawthorne* (Boston: Houghton Mifflin, 1883), 7:255–56.

26. John Swanwick, *A Rub from Snub* (Philadelphia: Printed for the Purchaser, 1795), 76.

27. Ibid., 79, 77.

28. *Trials of the Human Heart* (Philadelphia, 1795), xiii–xiv; hereafter page numbers cited in parentheses in the text.

29. Part I had appeared on January 8, 1795, as an answer to a brochure published in England by James Thomson Callendar, an attack on church and state which got Callendar arrested. Cobbett's "Bone to Gnaw" had relied chiefly on personal abuse of Callendar, which attack elicited a review by Smith in his *American Monthly Review*, which in turn was attacked by Cobbett in "A Kick for a Bite."

30. Evans's *American Bibliography* attributes these anonymous pamphlets to Swanwick.

31. The script of the play has been lost, but the lyrics and score are in the Library of Congress.

32. For biography, see Ernst C. Krohn, "Alexander Reinagle," *DNB* (1935); Charles Durang, *History of the Philadelphia Stage between the Years 1749 and 1855* (Philadelphia, 1868), 1:35; and Julian Mates, *The American Musical Stage Before 1800* (New Brunswick, 1962), 35.

33. See Vail, *Bibliographical Study*, for evidence that the play was also performed on June 19, 1795 for the Rowsons' benefit night.

34. Benefit nights were held annually to supplement actors' salaries; the actor honored for the evening could advertise and sell tickets in any way she or he chose and kept all proceeds from the evening's performance. Rowson apparently wrote her own production for each of her benefit nights, including roles for her husband in all of them.

35. The dancing for *The American Tar* was choreographed by William Francis.

36. Joseph Ireland, *Records of the New York Stage* (New York, 1866), 1:174.

37. See Vail, *Bibliographical Study*, 161.

38. Anon., "Theatrical," *Massachusetts Mercury*, April 21, 1797, n.p.

39. "In Vain is the Verdure of Spring," [Philadelphia]: G. Willey, [1797–98?].

40. "He is Not Worth the Trouble," written by Mrs. Rowson. Composed by J. Jewitt (Boston: J. Hewitt, n.d.).

41. *A Ballad Sung at the Theatres and Other Public Places in Philadelphia, Baltimore, New York etc. by Messrs. Daly, Williamson, Miss Broadhurst, M. Hodgkinson. Written by Mrs. Rowson. Composed by B. Carr* (Philadelphia); Printed and sold at the Authors Music Repository (Baltimore: J. Carr, and New York: J. Hewitt, [1798]).

42. "America, Commerce, and Freedom" (Philadelphia: Carr's Musical Repository, [1794]).

Chapter Four

1. Vail, *Bibliographical Study*, 32ff., and Frank Luther Mott, *Golden Multitudes: The Story of Best Sellers in the United States* (New York, 1947), 316.

2. Mott, *Golden Multitudes*, 316.

3. See Robert Winans, "The Reading of English Novels in Eighteenth-Century America, 1750–1800" (Diss. New York University, 1972), for a revision of Mott's contention that Richardson was America's first best-selling writer.

4. Mott explains that this novel did not appear on his list of twenty "all-time" best-sellers because improved record keeping made it easier to document later books and because improved advertising techniques and the growth of population made it difficult to compare eighteenth-century books to later ones.

5. See Vail, *Bibliographical Study*, 21 for a complete listing.

6. Ibid., 19.

7. See Francis Halsey, "Historical and Biographical Introduction" to *Charlotte Temple: A Tale of Truth* (New York: Funk & Wagnalls, 1905), xxxvi; and Henry B. Dawson, *New York City During the American Revolution* (New York: Printed for the Mercantile Library Association, 1869), iv.

8. William H. Crommelin to William Kelby, July 8, 1876, New York Historical Society, New York, N.Y.

9. H. S. B., no title, *New York Evening Post*, September 12, 1903.

10. Halsey's introduction to the 1905 edition (xxxiv–xxxv) describes this edition.

11. Copies of this play are located in the Library of Congress, Wash-

ington, D.C., and in the Regenstein Library, University of Chicago, Chicago, Ill.

12. Rowson's name does not appear in the Library of Congress copy. I have not seen the copy in the Regenstein.

13. Halsey, "Introduction," xxii.

14. Loshe, *The Early American Novel*, 12.

15. Carl Van Doren, "The Novel and the Colonies. The Influence of Richardson," in *Colonial and Revolutionary Literature*, vol. I of *The Cambridge History of American Literature*, ed. William Peterfield Trent et al. (New York: G. P. Putnam's Sons, 1917), 286.

16. Alexander Cowie, "The Beginnings of Fiction and Drama," in *The Literary History of the United States*, ed. Robert E. Spiller et al. (London: Macmillan, 1948), 177–78.

17. Leslie Fiedler, *Love and Death in the American Novel*, rev. ed. (New York: Stein & Day, 1966), 90–98.

18. "Introduction" to *Charlotte Temple, a Tale of Truth* (New Haven, 1964), 19–20.

19. Jayne Kribbs, Conversation, December 27, 1979.

20. Vail, *Bibliographical Study*, 33.

21. Henry Simpson, *Lives of Eminent Philadelphians* (Philadelphia: William Brotherhead, 1854), 86–88; and J. Thomas Scharf and Thompson Westcott, *History of Philadelphia, 1609–1880* (Philadelphia: L. H. Everts, 1884), 2:1695.

22. Scharf and Westcott, *Philadelphia*, 1695.

23. *Trials of the Human Heart* (Philadelphia, 1795), 3:55; hereafter volume and page references cited in parentheses in the text.

24. For a discussion of Rowson's use of language in this and other novels, see Dorothy Weil, *In Defense of Women*, 137–40.

25. Cathy Davidson discusses this phenomenon in "Mothers and Daughters in the Fiction of the New Republic," *The Lost Tradition: Mothers and Daughters in Literature*, ed. Cathy Davidson and E. M. Broner (New York: Unger, 1980).

26. Rowson loved to name her characters after a quality or virtue. See Weil, *Defense*, 126, for a discussion of this technique.

27. *Reuben and Rachel* (Boston, 1798), iii; hereafter page references cited in parentheses in the text.

28. Vail, *Bibliographical Study*, 32.

29. *Sarah; or, the Exemplary Wife* (Boston, 1813), iii; hereafter page references cited in parentheses in the text.

30. Nason, *Memoir*, 18–19.

31. Vail, *Bibliographical Study*, 33.

32. *Charlotte's Daughter; or, The Three Orphans: A Sequel to Charlotte Temple*. Boston: Richardson & Lord, 1828, 60; hereafter page references cited in parentheses in the text.

33. May, 1828; reprint, *The Uncollected Writings of John Greenleaf Whittier*, ed. Edwin G. Cady amd Harry Hayden Clark (Syracuse: Syracuse University Press, 1950), 15–58.

34. Vail, *Bibliographical Study*, 81–84, 87–90.

Chapter Five

1. The first American geography book had been published in 1784 by Jedidiah Morse who, like all geographers of his day, compiled information from previous sources. Morse had followed this first text with two others, one for college-level students and one for small children. The only other American book on the market was Nathaniel Dwight's *Comprehensive System of the Geography of the World* (1795), also aimed at younger students. See *Dictionary of American Biography*, s.v. "Jedediah Morse."

2. *An Abridgment of Universal Geography* (Boston, 1805), 15; hereafter page references cited in parentheses in the text.

3. Nathan Dwight's *Short System of Geography* as quoted in Clifton Johnson, *Old-Time Schools and School Books* (New York, 1904), 339.

4. Vail, *Bibliographical Study*, 27.

5. *A Spelling Dictionary* (Portland, Me.: Isaac Adams and West and Richardson, 1815), iii; hereafter page references cited in parentheses in the text.

6. Vail, *Bibliographical Study*, 33.

7. See Johnson, *Old-Time Schools*, 371.

8. *Exercises in History, Chronology, and Biography, in Question and Answer.* Boston: Richardson & Lord, 1822, 56; hereafter page references cited in parentheses in the text.

9. See William Charvat, *Literary Publishing in America 1790–1850* (Philadelphia, 1959), 45.

10. Vail, *Bibliographical Study*, 27.

11. *Biblical Dialogues Between a Father and His Family* (Boston, 1822), 2:95; hereafter volume and page cited in parentheses in the text.

12. See Nason, *Memoir*, 119–20.

13. *A Present for Young Ladies*, (Boston, 1811), 85; hereafter page references cited in parentheses in the text.

14. See her letter to an older student quoted in Nason, *Memoir*, 151.

15. James Neal, *An Essay on the Education and Genius of the Female Sex. To Which is Added, an Account, of the commencement of the Young Ladies' Academy of Philadelphia. Held the 18th of December, 1794. Under the Direction of Mr. John Poor, A. M. Principal* (Philadelphia: Jacob Johnson & Co. 1795), 30.

16. Vail, *Bibliographical Study*, 70.

17. *Miscellaneous Poems* (Boston, 1804), 1:97; hereafter page numbers cited in parentheses in the text.

18. Nason, *Memoir*, 133.

19. Vail, *Bibliographical Study*, 31.

20. *Monthly Anthology* I (1804): 611–12.

21. Duyckinck, *Cyclopedia of American Literature* (New York: Scribner, 1855), 1:502.

22. In *The Introduction to American Magazines: 1800–1810* (Ann Arbor: University of Michigan Press, 1969), 2–3, Benjamin Morgan Lewis listed twenty-three magazines that originated in Boston, 1800–1810. In 1800 Lewis found only fifteen magazines in the whole country.

23. Quoted in Lewis, *American Magazines*, 6–10.

24. *Boston Weekly Magazine*, April 30, 1803, 109.

25. Ibid., April 28, 1804, 55.

26. Nason, *Memoir*, 117.

27. *Boston Weekly Magazine*, December 24, 1803, 33.

28. Ibid., February 5, 1803, 61.

29. Ibid., May 7, 1803, 113.

30. Ibid., October 8, 1803, 207.

31. The controversies arose when singing schools tried to establish church choirs. Singing schools were usually held by itinerant or local musicians who rented a hall and gave lessons in the reading of notes and basic elements of harmony. Before the rise of such schools, the ability to read music in America had passed out of existence, and church music had reached a low ebb. When singing schools originated in the 1720s, people objected to them, objected to people learning to read musical notation, and opposed any change in their traditional hymns heretofore sung from memory.

32. *Boston Weekly Magazine*, January 22, 1803, 9.

33. See Frank Luther Mott, *History of American Magazines, 1741–1850* (New York: D. Appleton, 1930), 249. Vail, *Bibliographical Study*, 27, 86, claims Rowson was a frequent contributor to the *Boston Magazine*.

34. Vail, *Bibliographical Study*, 86, and Nason, *Memoir*, 114ff.

35. Joseph T. Buckingham, *Personal Memoirs* (Boston, 1859), 83–85.

Selected Bibliography

PRIMARY SOURCES

1. Novels
Charlotte: A Tale of Truth. London: William Lane, 1791.
Charlotte's Daughter; or, The Three Orphans. A Sequel to Charlotte Temple. To Which is Prefixed, A Memoir of the Author. Boston: Richardson & Lord, 1828.
The Fille de Chambre. London: William Lane, 1792.
The Inquisitor; or Invisible Rambler. London: G. G. J. & J. Robinson, 1788.
Mentoria; or the Young Lady's Friend. London: William Lane, [1791].
Reuben and Rachel; or, The Tales of Old Times. Boston: Manning & Loring, 1798.
Sarah, or The Exemplary Wife. Boston: Charles Williams, 1813.
Trials of the Human Heart. Philadelphia: Wrigley & Berriman, 1795.
Victoria, A Novel. In Two Volumes. The Characters Taken from Real Life, and Calculated to Improve the Morals of the Female Sex, By Impressing Them with a Just Sense of the Merits of Filial Piety. London: J. P. Cooke, 1786.

2. Dramatic Works
The American Tar, or the Press Gang Defeated. [Performed in Philadelphia June 17, 1796. Probably never published.]
Americans in England; or, Lessons for Daughters. A Comedy. Boston: n.p., 1796. [No copy known.]
The Female Patriot; or, Nature's Rights. Philadelphia: n.p., 1794. [No copy known.]
Hearts of Oak. [Boston: n.p., 1810–11. Probably not published.]
Slaves in Algiers; or, a Struggle for Freedom: A Play Interspersed with Songs. Philadelphia: Wrigley & Berriman, 1794.
The Standard of Liberty: a Poetical Address. Baltimore: n.p., 1795. [No copy known.]
A Trip to Parnassus; or, the Judgment of Apollo on Dramatic Authors and Performers. A Poem. London: John Abraham, 1788.
The Volunteers. Philadelphia: Printed for the Author, [1795].

3. Educational Writings

An Abridgment of Universal Geography, Together with Sketches of History. Designed for the Use of Schools and Academies in the United States. Boston: John West, [1805].

Biblical Dialogues Between a Father and His Family: Comprising Sacred History, From the Creation to the Death of our Saviour Christ. The Lives of the Apostles, and the Promulgation of the Gospel; with a Sketch of the History of the Church down to the Reformation. The Whole Carried on in Conjunction with Profane History. Boston: Richardson & Lord, 1822.

Exercises in History, Chronology, and Biography, in Question and Answer. For the Use of Schools. Comprising Ancient History, Greece, Rome, &c. Modern History, England, France, Spain, Portugal, &c. The Discovery of America, Rise, Progress and Final Independence of the United States. Boston: Richardson & Lord, 1822.

A Present for Young Ladies; Containing Poems, Dialogues, Addresses, &c. As Recited by the Pupils of Mrs. Rowson's Academy, at the Annual Exhibitions. Boston: John West, 1811.

A Spelling Dictionary, Divided into Short Lessons, for the Easier Committing to Memory by Children and Young Persons; and Calculated to Assist Youth in Comprehending What They Read. Boston: John West, 1807.

Youth's First Steps in Geography. Being a Series of Exercises Making the Tour of the Habitable Globe. For the Use of Schools. Boston: Wells & Lilly, 1818.

4. Poetical Works

Miscellaneous Poems. Boston: Gilbert & Dean, 1804.

Poems on Various Subjects. London: G. G. J. & J. Robinson, 1788. [No copy known.]

SECONDARY SOURCES

1. Bibliographies

Parker, Patricia L. *Early American Fiction: A Reference Guide.* Boston: G. K. Hall, 1984. [Annotated bibliography of critical works.]

Vail, Robert W. G. *Susanna Haswell Rowson, The Author of Charlotte Temple. A Bibliographical Study.* Worcester: American Antiquarian Society, 1933. [Lists editions of Rowson's works.]

2. Books and Parts of Books

Blakey, Dorothy. *The Minerva Press 1790–1820.* London: Oxford University Press, 1939.

Bowne, Eliza Southgate. *A Girl's Life Eighty Years Ago: Selections from the Letters of Eliza Southgate Bowne.* New York: Charles Scribner, 1888.

Brandt, Ellen Barbara. "Susanna Haswell Rowson: A Critical Biography." Ph.D. Diss. University of Pennsylvania, 1974.

Brooks, Charles. *History of Medford: 1630–1855.* Boston: James M. Usher, 1855.

Brown, Herbert Ross. *The Sentimental Novel in America: 1789–1860.* Durham: Duke University Press, 1940.

Buckingham, Joseph T. *Personal Memoirs and Recollections of Editorial Life.* Boston: Ticknor, Reed & Fields, 1859.

Charvat, William. *Literary Publishing in America: 1790–1850.* Philadelphia: University of Pennsylvania Press, 1959.

Clapp, William W. *A Record of the Boston Stage.* 1853. Reprint, St. Clair Shores: Scholarly Press, 1970.

Collins, A. S. *The Profession of Letters. A Study of the Relation of Author to Patron, Publisher, and Public.* New York: Dutton, 1929.

Dall, Caroline Wells. *The Romance of the Association: or, One Last Glimpse of Charlotte Temple and Eliza Wharton.* Cambridge: John Wilson & Son, 1875.

Dexter, Edwin G. *A History of Education in the United States.* New York: Macmillan, 1911.

Dunlap, William. *A History of the American Theatre.* 1797. Reprint, New York: Burt Franklin, 1963.

Durang, Charles. *History of the Philadelphia Stage Between the Years 1749 and 1855.* Philadelphia: University of Pennsylvania Library, 1868.

Fiedler, Leslie A. *Love and Death in the American Novel.* Rev. ed. New York: Stein & Day, 1966.

Hare, Arnold. *The Georgian Theatre in Wessex.* London: Phoenix House: 1958.

Hewitt, Bernard. *Theatre USA, 1775 to 1957.* New York: McGraw Hill, 1959.

Hogan, Charles B. *The London Stage, 1778–1800. A Critical Introduction.* Carbondale: Southern Illinois University Press, 1968.

Ireland, Joseph. *Records of the New York Stage.* New York: T. H. Morrell, 1866. Vol. 1.

Johnson, Clifton. *Old-Time Schools and School Books.* New York: Macmillan, 1904.

Jones, Edward Alfred. *The Loyalists of Massachusetts. Their Memorials, Petitions, and Claims.* 1930. Reprint, Baltimore: Genealogical Press, 1969.

Loshe, Lillie Deming. *The Early American Novel.* New York: Columbia University Press, 1907.

McNamara, Brooks. *The American Playhouse in the Eighteenth Century.* Cambridge: Harvard University Press, 1969.

Martin, Wendy. "Seduced and Abandoned in the New World: The Fallen Woman in American Fiction." In *American Sister-hood: Writings of the*

Feminist Movement from Colonial Times to the Present. Edited by Wendy Martin. New York: Harper & Row, 1972.

Mates, Julian. *The American Musical Stage Before 1800.* New Brunswick: Rutgers University Press, 1962.

Meserve, Walter J. *An Emerging Entertainment: The Drama of the American People to 1828.* Bloomington: Indiana University Press, 1977.

Mills, W. J. *Through the Gates of Old Romance.* Philadelphia: J. B. Lippincott, 1903.

Mott, Frank Luther. *Golden Multitudes: The Story of Best Sellers in the United States.* New York: Macmillan, 1947.

Nason, Elias. *A Memoir of Mrs. Susanna Rowson.* Albany: Joel Munsell, 1870.

Norton, Mary Beth. *The British-Americans: The Loyalist Exiles in England, 1774–1789.* London: Constable, 1974.

Rourke, Constance. *The Roots of American Culture and Other Essays.* New York: Harcourt, Brace, 1942.

Seilhamer, George O. *History of the American Theatre from 1774 to 1797.* Philadelphia: Globe Printing, 1891.

Singer, Godfrey Frank. *The Epistolary Novel: Its Origin, Development, Decline, and Residuary Influence.* Philadelphia: University of Pennsylvania Press, 1933.

Spargo, John. *Anthony Haswell: Printer, Patriot, Ballader.* Rutland, Vt.: Tuttle, 1925.

Tompkins, Joyce M. S. *The Popular Novel in England 1770–1800.* London: Constable, 1933.

Weil, Dorothy. *In Defense of Women: Susanna Rowson (1762–1824).* University Park and London: Pennsylvania State University Press, 1976.

3. Articles

Cutting, Rose Marie. "Defiant Women: The Growth of Feminism in Fanny Burney's Novels." *Studies in English Literature 1500–1900* 17 (1977): 519–30.

Dauber, Kenneth. "American Culture as Genre." *Criticism* 22 (Spring 1980):104, 106–9.

Davidson, Cathy N. "Flirting with Destiny: Ambivalence and Form in the Early American Sentimental Novel." *Studies in American Fiction* 10 (Spring 1982):17–39.

H. S. B. [No title.] *New York Evening Post.* September 12, 1903.

Halsey, Francis W. "Historical and Biographical Introduction to *Charlotte Temple: A Tale of Truth*, by Susanna Rowson. New York: Funk & Wagnalls, 1904.

Howay, F. W. "A Short Account of Robert Haswell." *Washington Historical Quarterly* 24 (1933):83–90.

Kable, William S. Introduction to *Three Early American Novels*. Columbus: Charles E. Merrill, 1970.

Kerber, Linda. "Daughters of Columbia: Educating women for the Republic, 1787–1805." *The Hofstadter Aegis. A Memorial*. Edited by Eric L. McKitrick and Stanley Elkins. New York: Knopf, 1970, 36–59.

Kerr, John N. "The Bankruptcy of the Chestnut Street Theatre, Philadelphia, 1799." *Theatre Review* 11 (1971): 154–72.

Kirk, Clara M. and Rudolf Kirk. Introduction to *Charlotte Temple* by Susanna Rowson. New Haven: College and University Press, 1964.

Knapp, Samuel Lorenzo. "A Memoir of the Author." *Charlotte's Daughter; or, The Three Orphans. A Sequel to Charlotte Temple* by Susanna Rowson. Boston: Richardson & Lord, 1828.

Mrs. Rowson. "To Her Friends and the Public in General." *Baltimore Telegraph*. November 26, 1795.

"Mrs. Rowson." *Columbian Centinel*. March 6, 1824.

"Mrs. Rowson's Young Ladies' Academy." *Columbian Centinel*. April 15, 1807, 7.

"Obituary of Susanna Haswell Rowson." *Boston Evening Gazette*. March 6, 1824, 6.

Sargent, Mary E. "Susanna Rowson." *Medford Historical Register* 7 (1904):24–40.

Scull, G. D., ed. "The Montresor Journals." *New-York Historical Society* 14 (1881):3–578.

"Theatrical." *Massachusetts Mercury*. April 21, 1797.

Watkins, Walter Kendall. "The Great Street to Roxbury Gate: 1630–1830." *Bostonian Society Publications*, 2d ser., 3 (1919):89–126.

Index

WORKS—POETRY:
"Eulogy to the Memory of George Washington," 20
"Mighty Lord, The," 121
Miscellaneous Poems, 115–18; reviews, 118
"Rights of Woman," 116–17
Trip to Parnassus, A, 9, 12–13, 61–67, 118–28
"Wedding Supper, The," 121
"Women As They Are," 47, 117

WORKS—PROSE:
Abridgement of Universal Geography, 21, 100, 103–7
Biblical Dialogues, 22, 110–11
Exercises in History, Chronology, and Biography, 22, 109–10
Present for Young Ladies, 22, 98, 111–15
Spelling Dictionary, A, 108–9

WORKS—SONGS:
"America, Commerce, and Freedom," 78, 82
"He Is Not Worth the Trouble," 152
"I Never Will Be Married," 152
"Independent and Free," 79
"In Vain Is the Verdure of Spring," 80
"Little Sailor Boy, The," 81
"Soldier Is the Noblest Name, A," 78
"Where Can Peace of Mind Be Found," 32
"Willy of the Dale," 81

WORKS (cont.): didacticism in, 28, 34, 37, 39, 40, 43, 45; epistolary form in, 28, 32, 45–46, 52, 88, 96; female villains in, 31, 54; filial piety in, 28, 38, 41, 43, 93; seduction in, 29, 30, 38, 43, 53–55, 58, 89, 101–2, 130; sea adventures in, 39, 58, 86, 101; sentimentalism in, 32, 34, 39, 40, 42, 43, 87, 94, 101; women as authors in,

25–26, 36, 38, 39; women, community of 29–30, 37, 89; women's appearance, 31; women's education, 43, 45, 47, 48, 55, 56, 59, 93, 112, 117 (*see also* Rowson as educator)

Rowson, William, 10–11, 12, 16, 17, 18, 19, 20, 21, 23, 27, 79
Rowson, William, Jr., 11, 22, 23, 81, 129
Rowson, William S., 23
Royalty Theater, 65
Rush, Benjamin, 74

Sadler's Wells Theater, 8, 79
Sailor's Landlady, The, 82
Shakespeare, 4, 64
Sheridan, Richard, 26, 61
Siddons, Sarah, 9, 27, 64, 73
Smith, Samuel Harrison, 73
Smollett, Tobias, 25, 157
Souther, Captain Daniel, 5
Southwark Theater, 14
Spargo, John: *Anthony Haswell,* 125
Stanley, Charlotte, 51
Sterne, Laurence, 25, 34, 38, 84
Submission, cult of, 28–29
Swanwick, John: *British Honour and Humanity, Rub From Snub, A Roaster,* 75–77

Taylor, Raynor, 16, 79
Thaxter, Samuel, 10
Theatre Royal, Edinburgh, 14
Topham, Edward, 61
Trinity Church, 84, 85
Tufts family, 20
Tyler, "Colonel," 17
Tyler, Royall: *Algerine Captive,* 68

Uncle Tom's Cabin, 84

Van Doren, Carl, 86
van Hagan, Peter, 16, 18, 80
Vail, R. W. G., 84, 85, 118